PRINT CASEBOOKS 10/
THE BEST IN COVERS & POSTERS

PRINT
CASEBOOKS 10
THE BEST IN
COVERS &
POSTERS

Written by
Julie Lasky and Tod Lippy
Published by
RC Publications, Inc., Rockville, MD

Introduction

First published in 1994 in the United States of America by RC Publications, Inc. 3200 Tower Oaks Boulevard Rockville, MD 20852

Manufactured in Singapore

First Printing 1994

PRINT CASEBOOKS 10/THE BEST IN COVERS & POSTERS (1994–95 EDITION)
Library of Congress Catalog Card Number 75-649581
ISBN 0-915734-93-1

PRINT CASEBOOKS 10 (1994–95 EDITION)
Complete 6-Volume Set
ISBN 0-915734-87-7

RC PUBLICATIONS
President and Publisher: Howard Cadel
Vice President and Editor: Martin Fox
Art Director: Andrew P. Kner
Assistant Art Director: Michele L. Trombley
Managing Director: Linda Silver
Cover Illustration: Brian Ajhar

Black-and-white dominated the covers selected for this Casebook—not merely the prevalence of two-color solutions with an accent tint here and there, but a kind of graphic and conceptual starkness exercised by designers who were willing to hang an idea on the line. Louise Fili's decision to flout the edicts of book publishing and put a monochromatic portrait of an African American on the jacket of *American Photography Seven*; Raymond Pettibon's cartoonishly menacing line drawings for Sonic Youth's *Disappearer* CD; and Scott Menchin's interpretation in pen-and-ink of a Philadelphia Inquirer Magazine story about a man imprisoned for his brother's crime are powerful examples of this trend, and yet none could be classified as the kind of low-impact project that risked nothing by maintaining a hard conceptual edge.

Indeed, the two Time magazine covers chosen by the Casebook jury were entirely market-driven, and both featured two-color art. An all-type cover that spelled out the word "Evil" in black on black was approved by one of the most conservative publishing establishments in existence. And Time would soon follow this anomaly with the cover that kicked off its 1992 redesign: the literal and metaphorical "negative image" of Bill Clinton, as neat a concept as has ever been printed in this age of polychromatic wizardry.

If changes are afoot in cover design—an easy supposition since change is usually afoot just about everywhere—the Casebook jurors believe that magazines have in fact changed little in the past several years relative to other design genres. "It's the category that has stayed the most traditional," Peter Good observed. "By their very nature, magazines are restricted because they have to do a certain thing. With books, you can get away with just a strong image."

In other words, while CD covers are winning awards in industrial design competitions, and posters are no longer being posted so frequently but covered with type the size of an ant's thorax and mailed to their audiences, magazines continue to compete for attention on the newsstand with scores of other publications, producing, at least in this writer's imagination, an image out of a Damon Runyon story: Time scuffling with Newsweek or getting sucker-punched by U.S. News & World Report; Vogue, Harper's Bazaar, Mademoiselle, and Allure in a big, girly brawl. Efforts to find fancy ways to upstage the competition have led art director Dwayne Flinchum, another Casebook juror, to lament that "700 magazines on the newsstand are killing quality." Says Good: "'Groundbreaking' is being confused with 'shocking' or anything unique. People think they can be outrageous by being obscure."

The conceptual elegance of many of the design solutions here may be a reaction to this visual cacophony. Oscar Wilde once joked about a continual fear of not being misunderstood, and the same could be said of covers more concerned with setting a mood than making a statement, or, God forbid, taking a risk. Very few publications on our Runyonesque newsstand, or in the scarcely more cordial bookstore environment, actually bloody their noses. For risk is not a pregnant Demi Moore undressed on the cover of Vanity Fair. (The magazine's former editor, Tina Brown, earned her reputation for brilliance by marrying sensationalism and sophistication under what looks like a teetering canopy of risk but is in fact one rock-solid *huppah*.) Risk is James Victore's design of the classic antiwar novel *Johnny Got His Gun*, which not only replaced a fine and familiar cover of the previous edition for Citadel Underground but did so with a photograph of a soldier drawn and quartered by a butcher's diagram. Risk is Tod Lippy's lowercase logo printed halfway down the front of his art magazine, Publicsfear. Set in 10-point italic, the logo is the only type on the cover and is totally obscured when the publication sits in the rack because Lippy hopes that his readers will be attracted to the full-bleed photographs printed on the front of each issue and will eventually find their way to the content and checkout counter. These are the only readers Lippy wants, in fact. Everyone else can buy Vanity Fair as far as he's concerned.

Extrapolating from the choices and comments of this Casebook jury, we may conclude that visual cacophony, is not confined to the

newsstand or bookstore display, but engrained in our design culture. One can fight it even when designing publications that do not have to compete for attention. Dartmouth Alumni Magazine, HMO, Boston Globe Magazine, Philadelphia Inquirer Magazine are either blessed with a subscriber-based circulation or else piggybacked onto a daily newspaper. And still we see covers that slice through clutter like ice-breakers nosing across the Antarctic. In the book-publishing world, the work of art directors and designers like Louise Fili, Steven Brower, Jackie Merri Meyer, and Carin Goldberg is built on strong thinking—and, one can imagine, given the interference of most marketing departments—equally strong spines.

The Casebook jury, after a half-day of judging the covers category, selected 16 book covers, 17 magazines, and 5 CD packages. I have not mentioned the role of digital technology in any of this work. Though many people, including certain members of the jury, believe the computer is at the root of esthetic muddle, I found its presence or absence irrelevant to the effectiveness of the solutions presented here. Of course, as issues regarding photomanipulation in journalism heat up, and as protean media continue to assume new guises, the computer will loom very large in these pages, endowing them with all its technical and ethical perplexities and mixing black and white into a thousand shades of gray. —*Julie Lasky*

The poster is only a means to an end, a means of communication between the dealer and the public, something like a telegraph. The poster designer plays the part of a telegraph official: he does not initiate news: he merely dispenses it. No one asks him for his opinion, he is only required to bring about a clear, good and exact connection.
—A.M. Cassandre, 1933
Although Cassandre's rather self-effacing definition of the poster designer's role may strike the Casebook reader as a bit dated, his fundamental point still holds true: Whatever else a successful poster may do, it always conveys the essence of its subject matter in a simple, direct, and dynamic way. Of course, the role of the designer has evolved considerably over the years: Most of the posters in this book result from an intensive collaboration between client and designer, if not autonomous creative efforts by designers themselves.

And the role of the poster has changed as well: Its once-unmatchable power has become attenuated in the second half of this century. Much of its efficacy as a communications tool has been bettered by television and, increasingly, other electronic media. It still reigns, however, in the city, where pedestrian traffic provides a captive, if often distracted, audience. Many of the works in this volume, in fact, were originally meant for bus shelters, building exteriors, and theater facades, from Seattle to New York. While most large corporations (similar in scale to those Cassandre represented

in his posters of the '20s and '30s) no longer depend on the graphic impact of a poster to sell their products, cultural venues, such as film production companies, theaters, museums, and universities still use poster designs to inform and intrigue urban passersby.

Of course, a fair percentage of the work shown here has a more narrow, at times almost intimate, focus. Many posters were created as mailers for very specific audiences, announcing speaking engagements, apprising other creatives of studio anniversaries, and even conveying personal political convictions. Some were produced in editions as small as 75, and hand-distributed. More than one was hand-printed by its designer.

Regardless of the scope of these efforts, however, almost all are in one way or another affected by two consistent factors: the computer and the economy. Only a handful of the winners were produced without any involvement on the part of computers (and in every case, proudly so); in almost every other instance, a Mac was used, even if only to set or distort type. More interesting, however, is the absolute dearth of any images that were totally computer-generated.

An unstable economy in many parts of the country (and world) had a notable effect on many of this volume's participants. Almost half of the winning posters were produced with "limited" budgets; several with hardly any budget at all. In these examples, such restrictions have hardly led to creative blocks. In fact, if

Photo by Lawrence N. Mayer

anything, a lack of funds seemed to force designers to rely less on the bells and whistles associated with big budgets—varnishes, hours on the Scitex, coated papers, unlimited palettes—and more heavily on a strong concept executed in novel ways.

This time out, designers used everything from crayons to butane torches to surmount the esthetic restrictions caused by financial limitations. Other innovative solutions were more subtle: One creative stayed within budget by approximating a four-color separation of a blue sky with only the cyan and black plates, and reduced the cost of a full-color sep of the rest of the poster's graphic elements by shooting them close to one another and then having the printer spread them out again for the final design. In another instance, the services of a photographer were rendered at cost with the agreement that the piece—with a simple switch of plates at the printer—would also be printed with different copy as a promotion for his business.

That ability to stretch a solution to its outermost limits, in a conceptual, practical, and esthetic sense, is what distinguishes all of the posters in this volume. At another point in his life, Cassandre referred to the poster as an "announcing- machine." As far as the winners of this Casebook competition are concerned, the announcement brings only good news: The art of poster design is alive and well.—*Tod Lippy*

Julie Lasky

Julie Lasky is managing editor of PRINT magazine and a freelance writer whose work has appeared in the New York Times, Art & Antiques, The Forward, and the Journal of the American Institute of Graphic Arts. She is co-author (with Steven Heller) of *Borrowed Design: Use and Abuse of Historical Form*. Lasky was educated at Wesleyan and Columbia Universities and worked as a book editor in New York City before joining PRINT's staff in 1989.

Tod Lippy

Tod Lippy is associate editor of PRINT magazine, managing editor of Scenario: The Magazine of Screenwriting Art, and the publisher, editor, and designer of Publicsfear, a semi-annual art and culture journal. He received his B.A. in history from Texas Christian University and master's degrees in art history and film from Williams College and New York University. He lives in New York City.

Carol Bobolts

Carol Bobolts is a founder and principal of Red Herring Design, a New York-based graphics and art direction firm specializing in entertainment graphics. Her clients include Atlantic Records, Elektra Records, Capitol Records, Warner Bros. Records, MCA Records, Associated Virgin labels, Island Records and various other corporations and ad agencies outside the entertainment industry.

Prior to founding Red Herring, Bobolts was employed by Atlantic Records and was responsible for Elektra Records packaging, merchandising and advertising. She was also with Pushpin Lubalin Peckolick and the Design Center of Cooper Union for the Advancement of Science and Art.

Her work has received awards from the Art Directors Club of Los Angeles, the Type Directors Club, Communication Arts, Chaumont Exposition Internationale des Arts Graphiques, CEBA and AIGA, and has been published in PRINT, Communication Arts, and Designing for Music. In 1990, she was nominated for a Grammy Award for Best Package Design.

Bobolts began her design studies at the University of Michigan and graduated from Cooper Union.

Steven Brower

Steven Brower is art director for Carol Publishing Group and the recipient of many national and international awards. His work has appeared in PRINT, Graphis, AIGA, the 100 Show and the Art Directors Club of New York annuals. He has served on the faculty of the Fashion Institute of Design and Merchandising in Los Angeles and is currently teaching at the School of Visual Arts.

Brower was raised in housing projects in Manhattan and the Bronx. He attended the High School of Music and Art, the School of Visual Arts, and California State University, Fullerton. He currently resides in southern New Jersey with his wife, Kati, and their daughter, Janna.

Dwayne Flinchum

Dwayne Flinchum, executive art director of Penthouse magazine, previously worked as art director for Omni magazine (1986–1992), and prior to that, as art director for a group of city and regional publications in the South, as well as a designer in a small corporate studio in Washington, DC.

A native of Virginia, Flinchum came to New York in 1984, where he soon won attention for his award-winning work at Omni. In 1989, he reformatted the magazine, and began providing graphic identities for new acquisitions at General Media, Inc., including Saturday Review, Science in the USSR, and Compute magazine.

As an independent, he has developed book jackets for Simon and Schuster, Macmillan, St. Martin's Press and McGraw Hill.

He has received awards from every major competition, including distinctions from the New York Art Directors Club and many trade publications.

He lives in New York City with his wife, Gina, and daughter, Alexandra.

Peter Good

Peter Good is an internationally known graphic designer and illustrator. His studio, Peter Good Graphic Design, works on various assignments for major corporations, small businesses and numerous arts organizations. This work has received awards from all the major graphic design institutions in the U.S. and has been published in graphic design periodicals throughout the world.

Since 1984, his posters have been included in all the Warsaw Poster Biennial Exhibitions, in each Lahti Poster Biennial Exhibition in Finland and two International Poster Triennials in Toyama, Japan, as well as in "Design USA," a cultural exchange exhibition sponsored by the U.S. Information Agency which toured Russia in 1990. His work is represented in the collections of the Library of Congress, the Cooper-Hewitt Museum, Die Neue Sammlung Museum in Munich, Germany, the Museum of Modern Art in Toyama, Japan, and Museum für Kunst und Gewerbe in Hamburg, Germany.

In October 1993, the four contemporary Christmas stamps Good designed for the U.S. Postal Service were released nationwide. The first day of issue of his design for the 1994 LOVE stamp was January 27, in Loveland, Ohio.

Good received a B.F.A. in graphic design from the University of Connecticut.

Index

**Magazines/Books
Albums/Posters**

**Clients/Publishers
Record Companies**

Carin Goldberg—one of America's most eminent book jacket designers—reports that she has received more compliments on this cover than on any other she has ever designed. "My most successful covers, design-wise and sales-wise, have usually been printed as intended," she says. And luckily, no one at Hyperion Books had the poor sense to interfere with her interpretation of Fae Myenne Ng's novel about a Chinese-American woman growing up in San Francisco's Chinatown, not even to right the upside-down *e* in the title.

Goldberg was handed the photograph of two young girls who represent sisters in the book, but thought the black-and-white image was "too journalistic-looking" and so tinted it a "pale, 'bone-like' color" to remove its nonfictional character. "I wanted the type to suggest a weathered, uncertain, or precarious message," she adds, explaining that the novel deals with an inter-familial struggle between old-world sensibilities and a young, assimilated generation. "The author's name was designed in the form of a traditional Chinese mark combined with clean, modern typography to reflect the 'Westernized' characters in the story."

Publisher: Hyperion Books, New York, NY
Art director: Victor Weaver
Designer: Carin Goldberg, New York, NY
Photographer: Genthe

A construction by the American Surrealist Joseph Cornell, who was famous for his boxed collections of strangely juxtaposed, lovely objects, was suggested by the author and editor of this novel, about a little girl who grows up to become a magician with her own children's TV show. "She has plenty of hidden secrets and treasures in her closet, and the Cornell piece illustrates this nicely," says Steven Cooley, of Harcourt Brace's in-house design department. "The typeface was chosen for its quirkiness and unpredictability, much like the main character."

Initially, Cooley had proposed reproducing the Cornell artwork as a full bleed and running type over the image. "The box contains a lot of interesting little elements that I wanted to show off as large as I could get them," he explains. However, Pace, the art gallery that represents Cornell, refused to allow the art to be obscured in any way, and Cooley decided to re-scale the work much smaller and incorporate textured paper as a background, rather than place the type in a narrow border above and below the image.

Cooley designed the jacket completely on a "souped-up" Mac IIsi, using QuarkXpress 3.1. The layout, with for-position-only artwork, was loaded into a Scitex system, and the Cornell image, along with the background pattern that simulates paper fiber, was stripped in by the publishing company's prepress house.

According to Cooley, the most interesting aspect of the design is the halftone spot varnish on the Cornell artwork, which lends a subtle texture, like the matte surface of a photograph. ("Unfortunately, it will not show up in reproduction," he laments.) The varnish proved to be the most problematic aspect as well: "The image area had to be separated as a halftone several times before a compromise was reached where the spot gloss area could hold the detail of the halftone."

Publisher: Harcourt Brace & Co., San Diego, CA
Art director: Vaughn Andrews
Designer: Steven Cooley
Artist: Joseph Cornell (courtesy Pace Gallery, New York, NY)

Below: early experiments with type and layout.

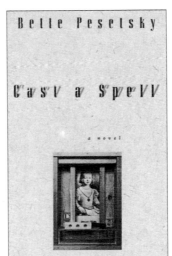

When Kevin Reagan, art director at Geffen Records, was asked to design four CD music samplers as promotional give-aways, he was offered virtually no time or budget. These constraints turned out to be wonderfully appropriate to the packaging of alternative music for a youthful audience (18- to 35-year-olds). To keep costs close to the bone, Reagan created one-color labels that were affixed to white cardboard sleeves containing a disk of recordings by Geffen bands, including Sonic Youth, White Zombie, and The Spent Poets. (The same disk was used in all four packages.)

"The entire project was done on the copying machine and pasted up by hand," Reagan recalls. "Some of the type was run out on the printer and then photocopied again to keep the whole rough look consistent. And most of the copy on the back cover was spliced and manipulated by hand."

Reagan was cheered by the thought of the generally poor quality of print on labels. To ensure that he would achieve a crude finished product, however, he further degraded the artwork by repeatedly applying a strip of Scotch tape and peeling it off. He drew some of the iconographic images and found others in a copyright-free book. "I didn't have much time on this, so I just pulled stuff that I could beg, borrow, and steal and put it all together," he says. The iconography might even have a mystical significance. Reagan recalls that "the night I finished the design of *Road*

Kill, I came home and there was a huge raccoon on my back deck like the one on the cover. It was very strange. I haven't seen it since."

The four titles of the sampler relate to the magazines in which each disk was distributed. *Spawn* is a play on Spin, *Road Kill* on Car Stereo Review, *Derails* on Details, and *Reflex Test* on Reflex, an alternative publication. The series of four disks was produced in an edition of 10,000 that rapidly disappeared through demand. "It was a real challenge to come up with an interesting yet very inexpensive solution—and the way I envisioned it from the outset came extremely close to the final outcome, a very rare experience," Reagan recalls. The project generated strong enthusiasm among the Casebook jurors, who unanimously voted it into the book.

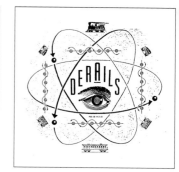

Client: Geffen/DGC Records, Los Angeles, CA
Art director/designer/illustrator: Kevin Reagan
Project coordinators: Rob Jacobs, Lori Baldwin

When the alternative rock band Sonic Youth put out an album called *Goo*, they requested that a friend of the band, the artist Raymond Pettibon, illustrate the cover. So it was only logical that when a single from that album, "Disappearer," was released by Geffen in digi-pak format (a compact-disk configuration that usually contains three to five songs), Pettibon contributed to this design as well. Recalls Geffen art director Kevin Reagan, "The band has a very distinct sound and vision. There was a definite look and feel we were after, and this package personified it completely. The cover was meant to be arresting. I chose this particular image because of its obvious impact and to reflect the 'alternativeness' of the music style."

Reagan's primary task was to maintain continuity with *Goo* while giving the digi-pak its own identity and making it attractive as a retail piece aimed at buyers, not merely as a promotional item. He was offered a larger-than-usual budget to accommodate the production of a three-color disk (normally, the disks he produces are two-color) and a special folding booklet inserted into the cover.

With the exception of a few lines of mostly legal-related type, Reagan designed the entire package conventionally, including the lettering, which Pettibon executed by hand and Reagan supplemented as necessary. "All art was black-and-white," he explains. "I added the second color to complement the intensity of

the drawings both in subject matter and style. I don't really know where the pink came from, but it worked." Reagan produced the mechanical by cutting and pasting photocopies or stats of the elements. The project was overseen and approved by the band, which is closely involved with all of its album designs.

Back cover.

Client: Geffen/DGC Records, Los Angeles, CA
Art director: Kevin Reagan
Illustrator: Raymond Pettibon, Hermosa Beach, CA
Letterers: Raymond Pettibon, Kevin Reagan
Printer: AGI, Chicago, IL

Lucy Bartholomay's covers for the Boston Globe Magazine demonstrate the art director's tendency to veer toward simplicity. "Especially when you are adding type to art, you need to leave room, both visually and intellectually, for the marriage of word and image," she comments.

Whether type dominates that marriage, as in a cover filled with the gripes of dual-career families, or is the more recessive partner, as in a cover whose headline curls like a mustache under a Terry Allen–illustrated nose, Bartholomay achieves the delicate balancing act week after week.

Both of the aforementioned designs were unanimous choices of the Casebook jurors, followed closely by a cover featuring illustrator Malcolm Tarlofsky's personification of an uninspired, misdirected Democratic party. "It wasn't so much the 'treatment' that was chosen, it was the artist," Bartholomay recalls of this work. "Malcolm's illustrations draw on images that push buttons for us. I knew his 'style' would help convey the attitude of the piece, which was both smart and offbeat."

Normally, Tarlofsky avoids the sketch stage and sends a single image to the art director. On this occasion, however, he faxed Bartholomay a sketch in which an engraved portrait of Teddy Roosevelt was blindfolded to convey a lack of direction, lobotomized to represent a dearth of ideas, and adorned with the Stars and Stripes "because politicians are great

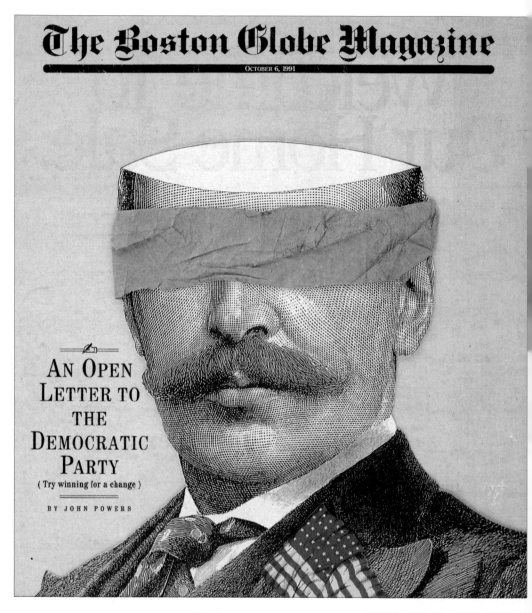

The Boston Globe Magazine

OCTOBER 6, 1991

AN OPEN LETTER TO THE DEMOCRATIC PARTY

(Try winning for a change)

BY JOHN POWERS

Malcolm Tarlofsky's original sketch, right, included a portrait of Teddy Roosevelt.

flag-wavers." A weathervane extending out of the head posed the question of where exactly the Democratic party was heading.

Bartholomay thought the blindfolded man with the empty head was a compelling enough idea and image without further additions, and she asked Tarlofsky to substitute a more generic engraved figure for Roosevelt. Once these simple changes had been made, she set the type in Aldus Freehand. "When you put the right illustrator with the right story, the process usually is effortless—it drives itself and something strong comes of it."

Bartholomay had a similar experience with illustrator Terry Allen in preparing a cover about the boom in 900 numbers. "The story did not have a point of view—it was a straight reportorial piece of journalism. The cover could have gone many ways. Terry wanted to have graphic fun and used '900' as a jumping-off point as well as a final design element," she explains. Bartholomay's only problem was designing the headline in a way that would not undermine the chemistry of the illustration and make the number unreadable. "I decided to go with very small type and actually use it so it looked like part of the illustration The cursive head becomes a mustache under the nose, and the drop-head and byline become the mouth. Terry reprinted this cover for a mailer and actually changed the headline into curved type. It now reads as a smile."

The all-type cover that

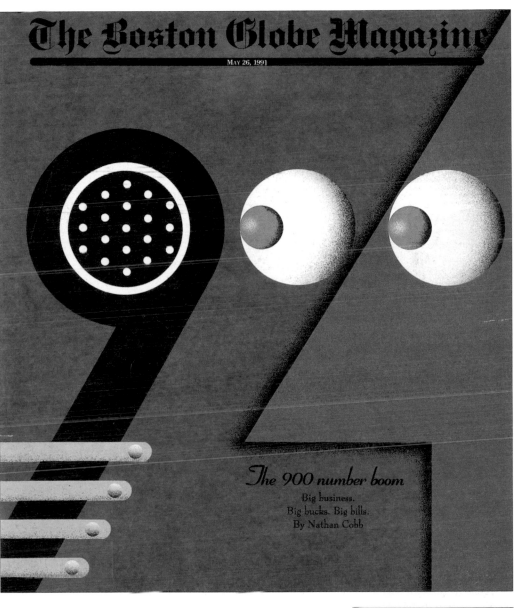

The 900 number boom

Big business.
Big bucks. Big bills.
By Nathan Cobb

Lucy Bartholomay designed the headline of this cover as a mustache complementing illustrator Terry Allen's face; Allen redesigned the headline as a smile for a promotion piece (right).

purports to tell "The Truth About Dual-Career Families" evolved out of a brainstorming session among magazine staff members to come up with all the daily complaints in families where both parents work. "We felt that this was such a hot issue with readers that merely stating the complaints would attract attention," Bartholomay recalls. "We wanted couples to sit around the kitchen table Sunday morning discussing this cover. It really is a typographic mirror of daily life."

Bartholomay points out that executing the cover would have been a copy-fitting nightmare without the Mac. Using Aldus Freehand, she was able to type all the copy in and rearrange it line by line so that the phrase "I'm too tired," repeated in red, could be placed and paced effectively in the block of black type. (The little illustrations are from a font called Cairo.) "I don't think I could have spec'd this cover for a type house if I tried," she admits. Nor could she have allotted herself only a day to produce it.

"The magazine achieved the desired reaction," Bartholomay says. "People were buzzing about it."

Publication: The Boston Globe Magazine
Art director/designer: Lucy Bartholomay
Illustrators: Terry Allen, Staten Island, NY (May 26, 1991), Malcolm Tarlofsky, Glen Ellen, CA (October 6, 1991)
Printer: Quebecor, Providence, RI

The Boston Globe Magazine

OCTOBER 27, 1991

I thought you were picking up the kids. Wait'll you hear about *my* day. We need some time alone. I'll pencil you in. What do you mean, *my* cat? I'm too tired. I was in a meeting. *You* pick up the baby sitter. Not takeout again. I'm too tired. Guilt is my middle name. I thought we talked last month. **THE TRUTH ABOUT DUAL-CAREER FAMILIES** Just because you make more money doesn't make you God. I'm not a mind reader. I'm too tired. Fine, *you* do the shopping from now on. If I make an appointment, will you pay attention to me? What makes you think I'm going to move? *You* have the baby. I'm too tired. So you vacuumed – big deal. When did you turn into my mother? *You* stay home and wait for the plumber. **BY ALISON BASS** I don't have time to be sick. I'm too tired. Those *can't* be chicken pox. What did I do to deserve children like you? My father never cooked. How do you feel about taking separate vacations? I'm too tired. Let me get back to you.

Favorite Families of TV

For the cover of *Favorite Families of TV: A Celebration of Twenty of the Most Popular Shows of the Past Forty Years*, Pentagram designer Michael Bierut came up with the idea of tiny, pastel-tinted headshots of TV-family members, including Ernie, the youngest sibling on "My Three Sons"; Ben Cartwright (a.k.a. "Pa") from "Bonanza"; and the eponymous "Beav" of "Leave It to Beaver."

Bierut's associate at Pentagram, Paula Scher, provided "stylistic guidance" and is surely responsible for the arrows that lend the illusion of a blood relationship between Robert ("Marcus Welby, M.D.") Young, Sally ("All in the Family") Struthers, and Larry ("Dallas") Hagman. (Years ago, Scher did a genealogical chart for the cover of PRINT magazine that hitched Sarah Bernhardt and Lucian Bernhard.)

Dorit Lev is credited with implementation, which involved QuarkXpress only in the final production art. The lettering was photocopied and pieced together from old typebooks.

The creative and unusual placement of the subtitle is a hallmark of covers designed under the auspices of Carol Publishing's art director, Steven Brower.

Publisher: Carol Publishing Group, New York, NY
Art director: Steven Brower
Design firm: Pentagram, New York, NY
Designers: Michael Bierut, Paula Scher, Dorit Lev

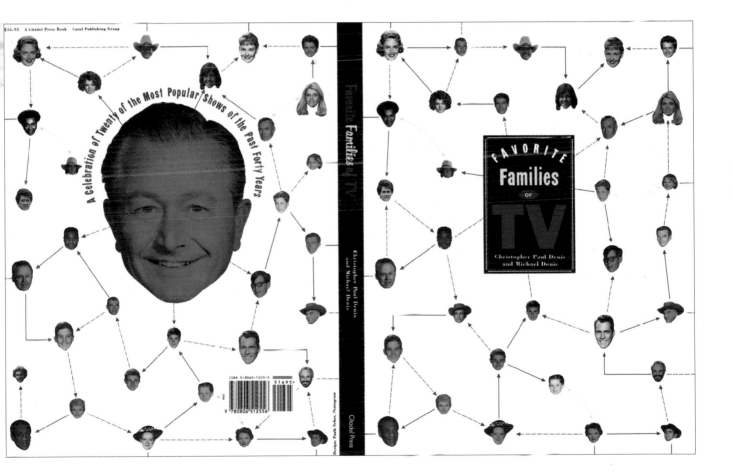

"*Sylvia*," explains designer Steven Brower, "is a mystery novel about a woman with a false identity and a tawdry past." And as if that weren't enough reason to blindfold the figure portrayed on the cover, Brower points out that the author, Howard Fast, was blacklisted during the McCarthy era and forced to publish this book (and others) under a pseudonym.

Brower's main concern was to evoke this double story while coping with his own identity crisis. Because he was the title's art director as well as designer and illustrator, he assigned himself his own budget, which involved doing the illustration at home for no extra fee. "The greatest limitation," he says, "was that the time spent painting was time spent away from my family. As a result, this piece is heavily imbued with guilt."

After completing the artwork, he scanned it onto a Macintosh IIcx computer at low (75 dpi) resolution to create a gritty, textural effect. "Since the monitor was black-and-white, I had no way to alter the illustration," he explains. "However, I do not feel the computer played a significant role in this piece. Had it been necessary, I would have achieved the same effect some other way."

Brower introduced the comp at a meeting with the president, publisher, editor, and head of sales at which he presented his entire list (about 80 titles). The only request was to make the author's name larger.

Publisher: Carol Publishing Group, New York, NY
Art director/designer/illustrator: Steven Brower
Printer: Coral Graphics, Plainview, NY

False Pretenses

For a refreshing departure from the clichés of the mystery genre, Jackie Merri Meyer, art director of Warner Books, commissioned designer/illustrator John Sayles to do the cover of a novel that revolves around women, guns, and Los Angeles detectives. Sayles's "retro" design style may recall the heyday of mystery writers Dashiell Hammett and Raymond Chandler, but the use of charmingly primitive line art and colors collaged like an Arp composition are not a common feature of contemporary thrillers. Indeed, the project was a departure for the designer himself, who had never attempted a book jacket before. Sayles confesses, "I really am not much of a fiction reader, and I don't like to get too close to my subject. On the other hand, my partner, Sheree Clark, loves an excuse to read something other than design stuff—so I had her read *False Pretenses* and 'interpret' the story for me."

Sayles took this opportunity to push his style to a point that was on the border of, but not quite beyond, recognition. He incorporated typewriter type partly to convey an informal feeling but also in revolt against the diversity of contemporary typographic choice: "You can get every font imaginable now, and it just seemed to be right for the project."

Meyer approved Sayles's initial comp, asking only that he enlarge the size of the author's name. She is also reported to have stuck up for the design against the advice of Warner's marketing department. "I think they didn't feel comfortable with it, and she refused to give in." Sayles says. "I'm glad. Everything we see these days is so stiff, with overlapped type on an arc or curve. I think this book will stand out more on a shelf for being different."

Left, top and bottom: Sayles's sketches for line art.

Publisher: Warner Books, New York, NY
Art director: Jackie Merri Meyer
Designer/illustrator: John Sayles, Des Moines, IA
Printer: Coral Graphics Services, Plainview, NY

"Judy, I know. . . . The one thing you didn't want was dead leaves!"

This was the message designer Les Kanturek faxed to Judy Doyle, co-director of Curbstone Press, along with sketches for the cover of a novel about a woman's poignant memories of her father. Yet, though he understood that his client was concerned about a too-literal interpretation of the story, Kanturek wanted to reflect the novel's elegiac and "earthy" tone and in some way illustrate the end of a colorful life. Leaves form the dominant image of the book (the narrator's father fantasizes that his last act will be to bury himself in a pile of leaves and die quietly as life goes on around him). And the image relentlessly captured the designer's imagination: Leaves appear in his sketches as bookmarks and borders and in patterns around picture frames, culminating in the falling leaf that bears the father's portrait.

Kanturek submitted a color comp before proceeding to the finish, but that was mainly a formality. "The solution made an instant connection with the client," he reports. "It just felt right. And it certainly fulfills my criteria for a successful cover: bold, simple, thought-provoking, and reflective of the contents of the book."

The illustration is a linoleum cut that Kanturek printed in black-and-white, hand-colored, marked with a China marker, and collaged with gray Canson paper. He hand-cut the type out of

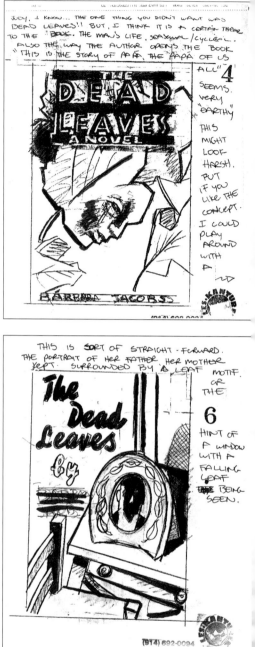

Above: sketches faxed by Les Kanturek to editor Judy Doyle reveal the designer's fascination with the literal motif of dead leaves.

linoleum, basing the main title on a typeface called Neuland, which he discovered in a book of Art Deco lettering. The type was done on a separate overlay to ensure an opaque black.

Above: Kanturek's comp features lettering based on an Art Deco typeface; below: sketch of leaf-portrait.

Publisher: Curbstone Press, Willimantic, CT
Art director/designer/illustrator: Les Kanturek, Middletown, NY

The most recent redesign of Time magazine was kicked off on April 20, 1992, with a cover so conceptually elegant it's a wonder no one ever thought of the concept before, a literal negative image of the president that illustrates "Why Voters Don't Trust Clinton."

As the Casebook jury revealed, however, inspiration didn't arrive at Time's shores with the redesign, but was foreshadowed in another effectively minimal cover, from June 10, 1991. That one had the audacity to feature a four-letter word in black on black, with no image. And yet, how better to communicate the headline, "Evil"?

"The story was an essay on the modern nature of evil, and we were trying to avoid cliché's," recalls Marilyn Salinger, a designer in Time's art department. Many versions, mainly classical paintings, were proposed by the art staff and editors before deputy art director Arthur Hochstein adopted a suggestion by Mirko Ilić, then art director of Time's international edition. "The cover story poses the question of whether 'evil' exists," Ilić explains. "The blackness of the background represents a fear of the dark, and the obscurity of the letterforms suggests the elusiveness of an answer to that question." (Salinger offers her own compelling interpretation, noting that the typography "suggests that evil lurks just below the threshold, where we can't see it.")

Designed in QuarkXpress, the cover posed the challenge

JUNE 10, 1991 $2.50

TIME

**Does it exist — or
do bad things just happen?**

of obtaining subtlety and clarity from a high-speed offset press. Ilić explains that Time's national edition is produced at only one printing plant, where printers were able to produce the typographic effects by using an extra run of black ink. International Time, however, is produced at seven different plants, requiring that the process be simplified to avoid an extra run. "Evil" created a stir on the newsstand, Ilić adds. It was one of the year's best-sellers and the subject of several articles in trade journals like Magazine Week.

As for the "negative image" cover, Salinger relates that this was "a fast-closing, late cover change," made two days before the issue went to press. Designed on a Macintosh IIci with QuarkXpress, the image was made from a color original that had been converted to a black-and-white negative in Adobe Photoshop. Salinger reports a strong reaction, both positive and negative, including subscription cancellations, but no reaction from President Clinton.

Publication: Time, New York, NY
Art directors: Rudolph C. Hoglund, Arthur Hochstein
Photographer: Steve Liss, Boston, MA

"Who is this guy? Just what is he experiencing?" These are the questions designer Beth Lee of Jackson Design hoped to invoke with the portrait that appears on the cover of *Shawl*, a CD by The Prayer Chain, an alternative music group. Lee explains that the face is not quite distinguishable because it was important to the band that no single member was showcased. Furthermore,

"This particular album had some ethnic influences," she relates, "from chanting to the kinds of instruments used in the songs. These influences led the art director, Buddy Jackson, to the idea of covering the band members in mud, a ritualistic experience that they really got into. When these images were presented to me along with the music, they led to the type

treatment as well as the photograph that appears on the back of the booklet."

Lee used QuarkXpress on her Mac IIci to set a small bit of type; the typography for the lyrics was hand-drawn by a band member who wanted to convey a personal feeling. The ghostly figures in the booklet photograph, portraying the band in a field, were created with Adobe Photoshop.

After being presented with four or five layouts "as well as plenty of opinions," which were reviewed with the band, the client selected this final version. Lee is generally satisfied with the outcome, but adds, "There's always something, isn't there? To a designer nothing can ever be really finished."

Top: front and back cover of CD; left: insert interior.

Client: Reunion Records, Nashville, TN
Design firm: Jackson Design, Nashville, TN
Art director: Buddy Jackson
Designer: Beth Lee
Photographer: Jim Herrington, Nashville, TN

When designer/illustrator Scott Menchin was asked to design a jazz CD produced by Stash Records, he recalls that the client was not particularly discriminating. "Only the names of the record and musicians had to go on the cover. Since it was mostly a mail-order company, the client didn't really care whether the type was big or small or bold or blue or red or to the left or up or down or jagged or serif or sans-serif."

Menchin settled on black letters, drawn in his own handwriting with the same bamboo stick he used to render the figure of trumpet player Art Farmer. ("I've drawn like this since I was 12, so I didn't see why I should stop now," he explains.) He then dressed Farmer in a photo-collaged jacket and tie, culling the "fabric" from an issue of GQ without being overly concerned whether the clothes bore any resemblance to something Farmer might have actually worn. A variation of the drawing appears on the back cover as pale blue line art on a bright yellow background—"real Warhol colors," the designer points out.

Menchin relied on the computer to produce type for the inside liner notes and back-cover song titles, identifying his tools as "the same as everyone else uses: Quark, with a touch of quirk."

Though he is disappointed with the production values, which he blames on the company's habit of gang-printing, Menchin found some consolation in the reaction of a friend who was impressed

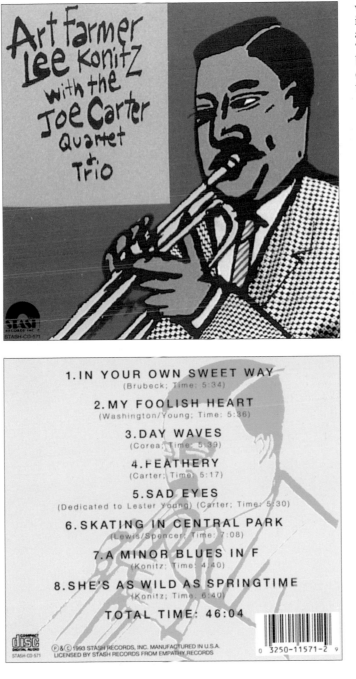

when he showed her the CD in a bin at a record store. "I'd also like to add," he says, "that in spite of the small budget and low production quality, I still get paid more than Art Chantry."

Client: Stash Records, New York, NY
Art director/designer/illustrator:
Scott Menchin, New York, NY

Art director Lloyd Ziff describes Travel & Leisure's May 1993 cover, which refers to a 24-page special section celebrating the American city, as one of the few "concept covers" the magazine had ever run.

The concept began with a sketch by photographer Geof Kern, best known for lyrical photo collages reminiscent of the early-century surrealism of Man Ray. Kern proposed photographing a boy who represents the youthfulness of the U.S. and demonstrates its free-ranging, future-oriented spirit by heading off along a country road in late afternoon light. Cradled in the boy's arms is a skyscraper, symbol of the American city, which Kern proposed rendering as a large color print that would look three-dimensional.

Ziff, along with photo editor Hazel Hammond and editor-in-chief Ila Stanger, preferred this idea to other of Kern's proposals, including a Fabergé-like egg that opens to reveal a variety of American buildings, and indigenous flowers whose blossoms are different kinds of regional architecture. "Part of the fun was writing the cover line to support the theme—'We'll Take Manhattan,'" Ziff recalls, "although there was some worry in the office that we were alluding to the then recent World Trade Center bombing. Luckily, that wasn't the building Geof used."

The reaction was immediately positive, Ziff says, adding, "I believe people will always respond to an idea much more than to a merely 'pretty' picture." The Casebook jurors agreed, giving this entry a unanimous vote.

MAY 1993 $3.00

TRAVEL & LEISURE

We'll Take Manhattan

L.A. and Boston Too!
AMERICAN CITIES:
THE GRIT,
THE GLORY

Publication: Travel & Leisure, New York, NY
Art director/designer/copywriter: Lloyd Ziff, New York, NY
Photographer: Geof Kern, Dallas, TX
Printer: Quebecor Printing, Arlington Heights, IL

"Designing for a trade publication, I have the great luxury of not worrying about newsstand sales," says Nancy Steiny, art director of HMO, a magazine for professionals in the managed healthcare industry. "The artwork can be more thought-provoking, and the cover lines can be reduced to a few, or only one." For a story featured in the May/June 1992 issue about using a computerized mapping program as a business tool, Steiny commissioned Malcolm Tarlofsky to combine a full-bleed sepia-toned photo with actual computer maps. She chose the photo-collage artist because he is "exceptional at solving difficult visual problems. And he combs sources for great 'scrap.' Also, he could incorporate the maps, which the client was interested in including."

Steiny used her Mac merely to design those sparse cover lines. "Once I am satisfied with the typography, the route is old-fashioned type set and then pasted on a board."

"It's an arresting, interesting image," she concludes. "My job is to get an executive's attention on a desk filled with demands. This succeeds very well, I think."

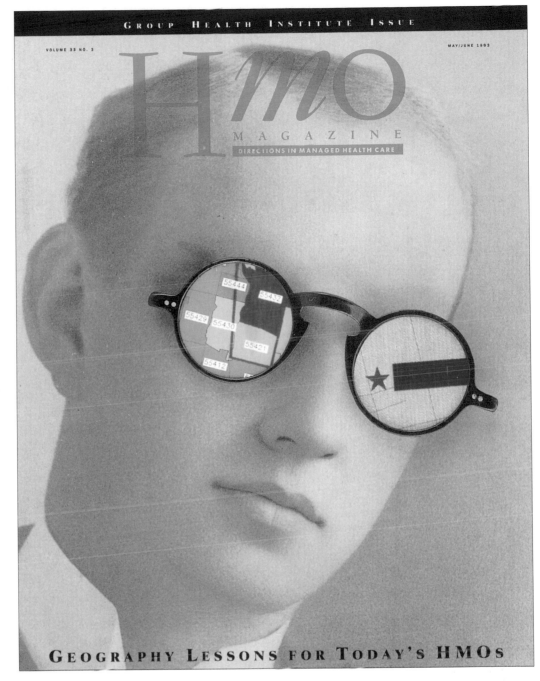

GROUP HEALTH INSTITUTE ISSUE

VOLUME 33 NO. 3   MAY/JUNE 1992

H*mo* MAGAZINE
DIRECTIONS IN MANAGED HEALTH CARE

GEOGRAPHY LESSONS FOR TODAY'S HMOS

Publication: HMO Magazine, Washington, DC
Art director: Nancy Steiny/Nancy Steiny Design, New York, NY
Photographer: Malcolm Tarlofsky, Glen Ellen, CA

In what is perhaps the first documented instance in Casebook history of somnabulant art direction, Jessica Helfand, recently of the Philadelphia Inquirer Magazine, recalls having had a vivid dream image, "at once nurturing and menacing," of one brother cradling another in a cage. The real-life inspiration was a story that was to appear in her publication about a man serving a life sentence in jail for a crime his brother had committed. Legal issues prevented the Inquirer from running photographs of the brothers, so it was fortunate that Helfand recalled her dream upon waking and translated it into an assignment for illustrator Scott Menchin, resulting in the art for "His Brother's Keeper."

"The idea, once visualized, seemed to reduce the story down to its most salient features," Helfand says. "The primitive style of Scott's drawing served to reinforce the content, recalling the relationship between the brothers, which had gone on since childhood. In an effort to keep that quality of the line drawing consistent, I asked Scott to pen the headline and subhead. It was his idea to place and draw the subhead as if it were hair."

The starkness of the concept and execution achieved exactly what Helfand had set out to do: draw readers' attention away from the many color commercial supplements stuffed into a Sunday newspaper. And it offered other advantages.

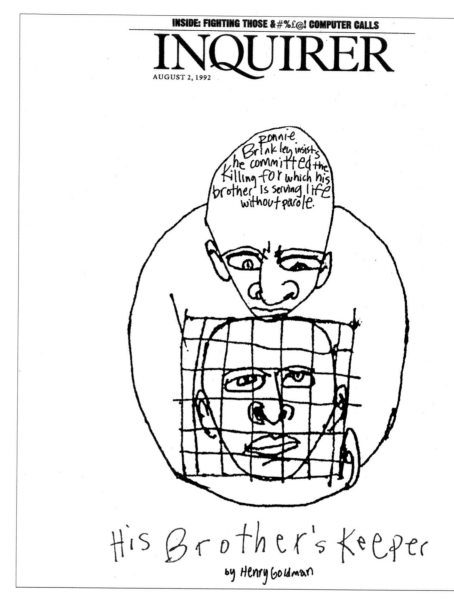

Notes Helfand, "Our limitations were primarily technical (rotogravure on newsprint; a huge run, which means no press checks) and political (working for a newspaper in a city with a fairly conservative audience).

The time frame, too, was a constraint. In this case, it all came together pretty flawlessly, and the lack of color allowed for fewer mishaps on press. After all, there was no real registration to worry about."

Publication: Philadelphia Inquirer Magazine, Philadelphia, PA
Art director/designer: Jessica Helfand
Illustrator: Scott Menchin, New York, NY
Printer: Quebecor Compucolor, Providence, RI

A unanimous selection of the Casebook jury, the April 1992 cover of Dartmouth College's alumni magazine owes its minimalism to editor Jay Heinrichs's desire for something direct, simple, and unconventional. The magazine is distributed to Dartmouth alumni nine times a year, and its captive audience allows the editorial and design staff to bypass most demands imposed by a retail setting.

For this story, which evolved out of a panel discussion by "experts" about the role of humor in culture, assistant art director Doreen Means used Adobe Illustrator to curve the type, including the parentheses, which resemble laugh lines, and the concept was executed just like that. "It's always fun to do something unexpected for myself, the editors, and the reader," explains art director J Porter.

Publication: Dartmouth Alumni Magazine, Hanover, NH
Art director: J Porter/J Porter Graphic Design, Peterborough, NH
Designers: J Porter, Doreen Means
Printer: Dartmouth Printing Co.

DARTMOUTH
ALUMNI MAGAZINE

APRIL 1992 • $3.00

(IS HUMOR STILL POSSIBLE?)

According to designer John Gall of Pocket Books, "This book is a wry six-month chronicle of the life of a 20-year-old member of the 'Benetton Generation' who travels around the world and collects shampoo. It is also a witty commentary on popular culture—things like rock videos, toxic waste, and eating disorders."

Because the publisher wanted to appeal to the same audience of 20- to 30-year-olds addressed (and chronicled) in author Douglas Coupland's first book, *Generation X*, Gall set out to produce a "quirky, fresh-looking design." The author himself had supplied a sketch, and Gall designed a

series of comps that followed Coupland's drawings more or less faithfully. He was primarily interested in interpreting the "Benetton Generation" theme, however, and the two final, printed versions—"male" and "female"—feature cropped color images, white backgrounds, and type reversed out of green bars, in humorous suggestion of Benetton advertising.

Images were scanned in on a Howtek Scanmaster 3 using a Quadra 900 and RasterOps 20" monitor with 24-bit color. Comps were printed on a QMS Colorscript 100 printer. The final mechanical was laid out on a Macintosh IIci, and

repro was output at a local service bureau. Final images were scanned and stripped in at the printer.

Though the responses both in-house and from the larger design community were favorable, Gall says he is not aware of whether the covers hindered or hampered sales. He does report that when the trade paperback version of the novel was published a year later, "It was insisted that globs of shampoo be added to the cover and that the green be changed to hot pink. I do not think these changes were necessary, and the response from other designers I spoke to was negative. But, hey, maybe shampoo globs sell!"

Top: author Douglas Coupland's sketch; below: series of comps designed by John Gall.

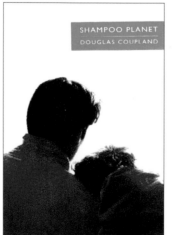

SHAMPOO PLANET

DOUGLAS COUPLAND

THE NEW NOVEL BY THE AUTHOR OF *GENERATION X*

SHAMPOO PLANET

DOUGLAS COUPLAND

THE NEW NOVEL BY THE AUTHOR OF *GENERATION X*

Above: "Male" and "Female" versions of final cover; left: trade paperback version with shampoo globs.

Publisher: Pocket Books, New York, NY
Art director: Barbara Buck
Designer: John Gall
Photographer: Sigrid Estrada. New York, NY
Printer: Phoenix Color Corp., Long Island City, NY

I Been in Sorrow's Kitchen and
Licked Out All the Pots

When designer/illustrator Michael Schwab was asked to do a book-jacket illustration of an African American woman struggling with poverty, he read part of the manuscript and developed a picture in his mind of a character worn to thinness by deprivation, someone frail and sad. He hired a model from an agency— "a thin, glamorous woman"—for a series of Polaroid photographs used as reference. But when he showed his sketches to the publisher, Hyperion Books in New York, he was told that the woman should be larger and sturdier.

Schwab had no need to return to the modeling agency: "There was a wonderful woman who worked at my neighborhood cleaners, and I asked her to come to my studio and pose for me, and she was perfect." Using this new set of Polaroids, he created a powerful figure whose strength is enhanced by a low perspective. The blackness of skin and shadow is complemented by vibrant colors (a total of six pure colors, including fluorescent yellow, were used in printing), and the solidity of the image is offset by the spindly lettering Schwab drew by hand with a stick dipped in paint. Readers were drawn to the poster-like simplicity of this cover. Indeed, the publishers received so many requests for a poster, they ultimately produced one.

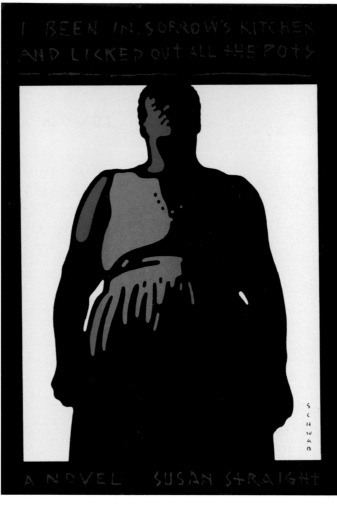

Publisher: Hyperion Books, New York, NY
Art director: Victor Weaver
Designer/illustrator: Michael Schwab, Sausalito, CA

Right: Polaroid images shot as reference. The top two photographs feature a model who worked at a dry-cleaning store in Schwab's neighborhood. The model in the lower two photographs was hired from an agency.

Working with zero budget, complete creative freedom, and a pile of jury-selected images, Louise Fili had only two requirements in designing the cover of this photography annual—to create something striking and graphic, and to do the job within a week so that the cover could be presented at a sales conference.

Neither stipulation turned out to be a problem. The lack of client interference (editor Edward Booth-Clibborn traditionally offers creative control in lieu of a design fee) allowed the job to run smoothly, and Fili had the chance to address "all of the inane and pointless edicts enforced by sales departments of publishing companies, which I have had to endure over the course of many years." Among the "rules" she flouted: "Never show a black person on a book cover" and "never run type up the side."

The Kurt Markus photograph Fili used was chosen because it was "very arresting, and since it was part of a series, we had another counterpoint for the back." Besides, Fili adds, a black-and-white image was a refreshing change for a photography book jacket. This piece was a unanimous choice of the Casebook jurors.

Client: American Photography, New York, NY
Art director/designer: Louise Fili, Louise Fili Ltd., New York, NY
Photographer: Kurt Markus, Kalispell, NY
Printer: Dai Nippon, New York, NY

Several months after the Los Angeles riots, an article appeared in the Atlantic Monthly proposing that competition between African Americans and Hispanics for jobs had been overlooked as a source of tension by the media, which was then spending most of its energies focusing on the clash between blacks and whites. "The article was written in a very straightforward way and was powerful not just for its excellent reporting but for its almost personal feel," recalls art director Judy Garlan. "I felt the art and the typography needed a power that was equally expressive and direct."

When Garlan saw a black profile painted by illustrator Karen Barbour in an *American Illustration* annual, she knew that she had found the "stark, timeless, and proud" feeling she wanted. She called the artist, suggesting a simple "face-off" between black and brown visages, and Barbour responded with sketches and a series of final versions. "Her paintings are really striking in person; they barely contain themselves on huge sheets of paper," Garlan reveals. "The way she works reminds me of when I studied Chinese calligraphy, where I would do thousands of simple brushstrokes attempting to make a perfect letter *A*, which in Chinese is just a single straight line. That fresh quality takes more tries, sometimes, then you'd guess."

Garlan selected her favorite brown head, but felt that the best black one was the painting she had originally seen in the annual (it had not

been previously published). "So often, the first dashed-off or spontaneous attempt has so much more energy than more polished versions. I've always been happiest when I've realized this and gone back to that energy—even if it means running a sketch rather than a 'final' piece," she says. The black head was ultimately flopped to fit Garlan's ideal composition.

Associate art director Robin Gilmore-Barnes chose the type (Modula and Erbar) and created the border using opaque film to echo the style of the art. Garlan selected a metallic ink, PMS 8601, for the logo and border so that the colors would oscillate between black and brown depending on the light.

Main headlines are usually set at the top of the magazine's cover, and Garlan recalls that editor William Whitworth initially objected to her suggestion to put the type across the faces, low down. She and Gilmore-Barnes eventually worked up a compromise by enlarging the subhead, so that the story's theme would be visible on the newsstand. As it turned out, Garlan says, newsstand sales were good.

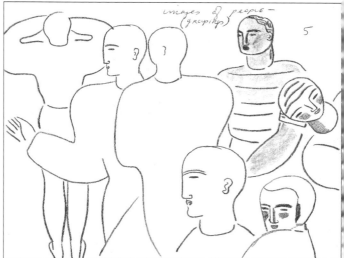

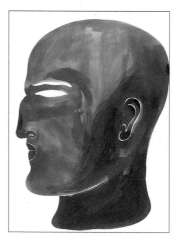

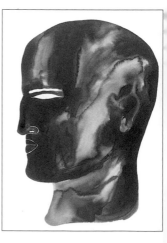

Opposite page, top and middle: Karen Barbour's initial sketches of immigrant groups; opposite page and this page, bottom: paintings of heads for use in the "face-off" solution.

VOL. 270 NO. 4

OCTOBER 1992

The Atlantic

ANTHONY BURGESS ON D. H. LAWRENCE / A VISIT WITH BILL CLINTON

IMMIGRATION AND THE NEW AMERICAN DILEMMA

BY JACK MILES

BLACKS VS. BROWNS

$2.95

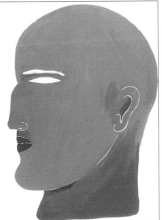

Publication: The Atlantic Monthly, Boston, MA
Art director: Judy Garlan
Illustrator: Karen Barbour, Iverness, CA
Printer: World Color Press, Covington, TN

For the first issue of the innovative art and culture magazine Publicsfear, Tod Lippy used an image by photographer Andrew Bush to convey the sense of urban anomie that informs the publication's content and gives it its name.

Lippy first saw Bush's work at an exhibition at the Metropolitan Museum of Art in New York. "I was impressed by the power of Andy's photographs of people in their cars on the Los Angeles Freeway. What he accomplished was literally a drive-by shooting. Both this image and the one on the back cover struck me as metaphors for individuals' inability to maintain a private space, forcing them to withdraw into tense interior environments."

The budget for this and subsequent issues of Publicsfear was excruciatingly small. Yet, like all of Lippy's artists and writers, Bush donated his work because he was impressed with the magazine's visual and editorial quality.

Lippy placed the lower-case Futura italic logo underneath the door handle out of rebellion against the design edicts of magazines sold on the newsstand. The small size, low position, and absence of any other cover lines ensured that viewers would be compelled to open the publication on the strength of the image alone.

Publicsfear, published twice yearly, has continued to feature the work of photographers on front and back covers with the same 10-point logo.

Client: Publicsfear Press Ltd., New York, NY
Editor/art director: Tod Lippy
Photographer: Andrew Bush, Los Angeles, CA
Printer: Preebro Printing, Brooklyn, NY

Inform is a membership
publication of the Virginia
Society of the American
Institute of Architects. Its
primary readership comprises
persons interested in
architecture, design, and
the arts.

For a feature article about
the design of the Children's
Art Resource Center at the
Virginia Museum of Fine Art,
a classroom for hands-on
experimentation, art director
Robert Meganck incorporated
a photograph whose red-and-
green palette harmonizes with
the logo created in Aldus
FreeHand.

Blessedly relieved of cover
lines that burden even
magazines directed to
specialized arts communities,
this cover announces its
contents in miniature sans-
serif type running along the
bottom. The informality is
reflected in the logo and
unobtrusive dateline and price
tag, leaving nothing to
compete with the strikingly lit
full-bleed photograph.

inform

architecture ■ design ■ the arts

march/april 1991 four dollars

Children's Art Resource Center ■ Business Interiors ■ Garden Archaeology ■ MESDA ■ Mill Town Architecture in Danville ■ Pioneer Women Architects

Client: Virginia Society of the
American Institute of Architects,
Richmond, VA
Art director: Robert Meganck/
Communication Design, Richmond,
VA.
Designers: Robert Meganck, Bill
Cullen, Tim Priddy
Photographer: Prakash Patel,
Washington, DC
Printer: St. Croix Press, New
Richmond, WI

Richard Solomon has a reputation for producing elite promotion pieces to showcase a crew of illustrators including John Collier, Gary Kelley, C.F. Payne, and Mark Summers. Maintaining these standards while producing an arresting yet affordable promo was the challenge handed to designer Louise Fili. "The original concept was totally different and actually more elaborate," Fili recalls, declining further description because she hopes to implement that concept in the future. "This version was an alternate proposal selected for financial reasons, though, obviously, with the foil-stamping and die-cutting it was not inexpensive to produce."

According to Fili, the cover of the book had to show work either by all of the illustrators, or by none. She chose none, preferring to design her piece around Solomon's logo, which had been introduced with his earlier promo book and is now a recognizable icon in the industry.

The initial comp was created out of two pieces of illustration board, red and black, glued together. No printer could simulate the effect, so Fili ended up working with a black and red cover stock of a much lighter weight than the comp material. The idea of foil-stamping so large an area was daunting to most printers, who doubted that they could achieve even coverage, Fili recalls. Ultimately, she found one who could solve the problem. She removed the hand that appears in the original logo partly because it would have been cropped in its position in the

Above: promotion cover features die-cut eyes and a hangtag; right: previous promotion introduced Solomon logo; opposite page: inside cover with type spiral.

corner of the book and might have become unrecognizable, but also because after experimenting with holding the book in different ways, she realized that it would get fingerprinted.

Fili worked on this project shortly before buying her own computer, so the cover illustration was completely manipulated by hand. "Here, the main challenge was getting the die-cut eyes to align with the *O*'s of 'Solomon' on the inside page. My determined assistant, Lee Bearson, did major facial surgery over the course of several days to make it work. The binding, of course, was extremely critical so as not to show any other letters peeking through the eyes." All this would have been accomplished manually even if she had had a computer, Fili says. Yet she is grateful that the spiral of type on the inside page was accomplished digitally with her typesetter's system, saving a great deal of time and expense.

Not least among her difficulties, Fili observes, is that "the book is received by thousands of art directors and art buyers who are inundated with similar materials. "Since we knew that the package would be opened, briefly perused, and, stuck on a bookshelf and lost with other promos, we needed an instant ID—thus the hangtag." These were hand-tied to each book.

"It was a challenge to go from the comp to the printed piece," Fili says, "but I was very satisfied ultimately." The Casebook jurors expressed their own satisfaction with a unanimous vote.

Client: Richard Solomon, New York, NY
Art director/designer: Louise Fili, Louise Fili Ltd., New York, NY
Printer: Terwilliger, New York, NY

A Casebook perennial, Mississippi Mud is the creation of Joel Weinstein of Portland, Oregon, who performs every artistic, editorial, and business function involved in putting out the 25-year-old publication, down to designing the ads.

Although the magazine, whose name derives from an old Tin Pan Alley song, is mainly devoted to literature and the arts, Weinstein's vision is broad; he defines his interest as life in America at the end of the 20th century. Each issue has an unstated theme to which the writing—culled from fiction and poetry the editor receives over the transom—may relate only obliquely, and too subtly for many readers to recognize. As for the artwork, Weinstein says, "I tell the artists—whose work is all commissioned for the issues—what I have in mind in the way of a 'theme' and hope that they respond to that as well as to whatever writing they're working with."

Weinstein continues, "I try to make the covers colorful, energetic, ironic, and somewhat disturbing, like the contents." For the "Mountebank Blowjob" issue selected by the Casebook jury, Weinstein told artist Eric Stotik that he wanted his work to relate to demagoguery and hysteria, "the prevailing moods of the day." Stotik's other tasks were standard operating procedure for the magazine; he was asked to supply two pieces of art, for the front and back covers, in a month's time and to expect minimal compensation—$150

for one-time use. "Because of the magazine's good reputation, I was confident of getting quality work," Weinstein says. When the art came in, however, it bore the wrong proportions for the full bleed he had anticipated, and Weinstein had to devise borders.

"I was pleased with my solution," he recalls. "The colored bands frame the art in an understated way, picking up its dominant colors without calling attention to themselves and balancing one set of proportions—the art—with another—the cover."

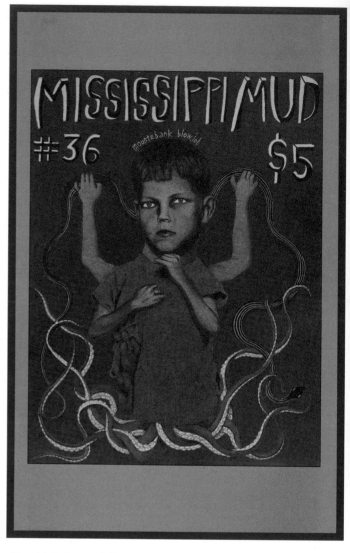

Above, left: back cover of "Mountebank Blowjob" issue; above, right: front cover.

Publication: Mississippi Mud, Portland, OR
Art director/editor: Joel Weinstein
Illustrator; Eric Stotik
Printer: Adprint Co.

For a nonfiction account of a mother's experiences coping with an autistic child, Michael Bierut of Pentagram in New York designed a cover that graphically alludes to disrupted communication. Interpreting illegibility as the graphic analogue of silence, he obliterated portions of the title with an airbrush so that the parts that remained emerge vividly out of the deep black background. "Century Schoolbook is the typeface that a lot of us learned to read with and subconsciously associate with childhood learning," Bierut explains. "We obfuscated it to give the viewer or reader a sense of the dislocation that characterizes the autistic experience, though obscuring the letters was actually harder to do than we thought. The production people at Knopf were concerned that we would make the words too illegible, and there was a continual process of going back and forth between dark and light."

Originally conceived as the dominant typographic element because of its hopeful message, the subtitle, "A Family's Triumph Over Autism," was ultimately set in small, fully legible letterforms that convey a fitting conclusion to both the story and the jacket. The cloud pattern in the bottom border is another signifier of hope, Bierut says. Art director Carol Devine Carson and her Knopf colleague Barbara De Wilde approved an early black-and-white sketch before Bierut proceeded to the finish, and they designed the jacket's spine.

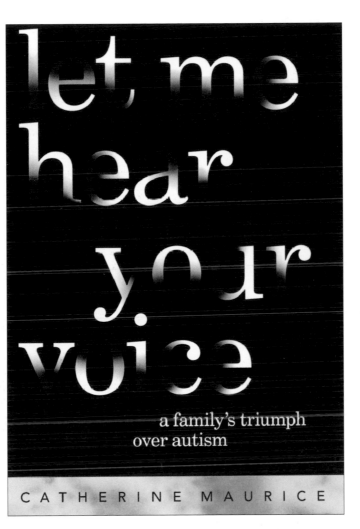

Publisher: Alfred A. Knopf, New York, NY
Art director: Carol Devine Carson
Design firm: Pentagram, New York, NY
Designer: Michael Bierut

For a boxed collection of blues guitar music by the late Elmore James, Warner Bros. Records art director Kim Champagne designed a witty ensemble of longbox, booklet, and CD inserts. The music was "for the most part recorded in a very spontaneous and primitive manner," explains Champagne, and she reached for the same spirit of rawness in her design. Part of the strategy involved hiring Josh Gosfield, a New York–based illustrator whose energetic collage style bears allusions to urban graffiti, to render images that appear on the front and back of the longbox and are repeated on the booklet and (in detail) on one of the CD inserts. Few photographs exist of James, so illustration was an obvious solution. More important, Champagne was looking for a way of encompassing the musician's life and work at a glance. "Being that Elmore James is no longer with us," she explains, "I wanted the cover to capture aspects of his personality, passion for his music, simplicity of his life, and the traveling he did playing in various blues clubs of the time."

Gosfield had to make time in a busy schedule to work on this assignment, but was interested enough to fit it in. Part of the bargain was that Champagne had to shop around in rare guitar shops to find a guitar that resembled one James might have used and send it to Gosfield by Federal Express to be painted. The original art was ultimately bought by the client, Capricorn Records.

After Gosfield completed and photographed his collages, the artwork, along with photographs supplied by the client, was scanned in at low resolution and used to lay out the booklet. Champagne had originally done a rough comp of the booklet by hand and had sent it to designer Mike Diehl for translation into QuarkXpress. Diehl used Photoshop to retouch photos that required background extensions, fades, and the like, for viewing purposes, and provided laser printouts, which Champagne corrected. Final output was supplied to the color separator on disk, along with artwork that had been polished by an actual retoucher. The jewel box inserts and inlay cards and CD labels were designed on the Mac in QuarkXpress as well.

Top, right: Kim Champagne's rough comp of booklet spread; bottom, right: Mike Diehl's computer translation.

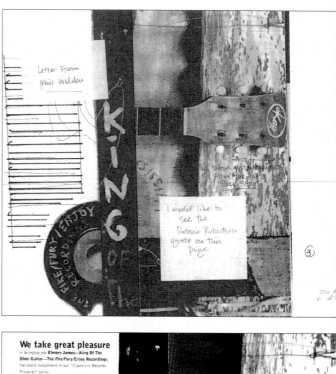

Client: Capricorn Records, Nashville, TN
Art director/designer: Kim Champagne/Warner Bros. Records, Burbank, CA
Designer: Michael Diehl/ Los Angeles, CA
Photographer (Elmore James): George Adins, courtesy Robert Sacre
Illustrator: Josh Gosfield, New York, NY
Printer: Ivy Hill, Los Angeles, CA

Top: CD package, including longbox, jewel boxes, and booklet; above: Josh Gosfield's 3-D compositions with hand-painted guitar; right: final image on longbox.

Words and Shadows

For a book about literature adapted for the cinema, designer Louise Fili bypassed the publisher's reference—still images from the movies mentioned in the text—and came up with the concept of a typewriter with a film reel in place of a ribbon. On the advice of photographer Ed Spiro, to whom she explained her idea and the need to work quickly and on a budget, she bought a used manual typewriter for $65 and handed it to Spiro to shoot. The resulting oversized black-and-white print was given to a retoucher who converted the ribbon into a film reel, sprocket holes and all. "The type was, naturally, typewriter type from an old manual," Fili recalls. "I tried to keep the size relative to the machine, though the publisher asked for it bigger (of course!)." Not only does this bold, direct solution veer off from the typical film book treatment, but its photographic realism is a departure from Fili's usual style.

Publisher: Carol Publishing, New York, NY
Art director: Steven Brower
Designer: Louise Fili, Louise Fili Ltd., New York, NY
Photographer: Ed Spiro, New York, NY
Retoucher: Ralph Wernli

Dalton Trumbo's novel *Johnny Got His Gun* is the monologue of a soldier who has been horribly maimed in World War I. "This is a very strong, poetic outcry for the end of war," designer James Victore explains. "My cover was intended to match the intensity of the emotion."

Assigned a normal budget, Victore, who also designed the series of which this volume is a part, chose not to exhaust it, finding the most power in a simple documentary photograph overlaid by the sort of diagram butchers use to show the different cuts of a slaughtered animal.

His solution succeeded to the extent that the publishers initially found the cover "too strong." They were especially disturbed by Victore's selection of black-and-white and by his use of a photograph of an infantryman on Hamburger Hill in Vietnam, which struck them as anachronistic, even though the book is viewed as a timeless antiwar statement. The cover was approved only after art director Steven Brower and editor Daniel Levy (who had by then left the company) confronted Carol's president at a meeting of the American Booksellers Assocation and convinced him to print Victore's design in a limited run. Says Victore, "It would have been wrong—ethically—to have bowed to a 'lighter' or merely decorative cover for such a book."

Publisher: Citadel Underground/Carol Publishing Group, New York, NY
Art director: Steven Brower
Designer: James Victore, New York, NY
Printer: Phoenix Color, New York, NY

As the Casebook jurors made their selections on tally sheets marked with numbers corresponding to each entry, one juror remarked that he wished he could have a sheet labeled "Rolling Stone" with dozens of numbers for him to circle.

Younger music publications, like Vibe and Ray Gun, may have invaded Rolling Stone's turf, but this biweekly of the rock-and-roll generation has shown a longevity and consistency few magazines in the industry are likely to match. Under the stewardship of art director Fred Woodward, Rolling Stone treats typography and photography as eminently renewable resources. If anything, observed another juror, Rolling Stone's covers are improving, having only recently begun to match the consistent excellence of the magazine's interior spreads.

The covers selected by this Casebook jury look complementary in their color schemes and in fact, according to deputy art director Gail Anderson, reflect the art department's taste for sepia, red, and gold. The big debate regarding the March 4, 1993, cover featuring rock star Bono was whether to use a Charles Burns illustration or a four-color black-and-white shot by Andrew MacPherson. "They were two incredibly strong choices and you really couldn't go wrong either way," Anderson observes. "The Burns illustration ran inside and made a fantastc spread."

Regarding the Bono cover, Anderson alludes to the "struggle with trying to squeeze in lots of cover heads in a pretty tight space and still be able to do something different and exciting." The solution in this case was red and black Champion, a sans-serif typeface, outlined in gold that runs vertically and horizontally in different directions, resembling a concert ticket.

Abundant verbiage was not a problem in designing the February 18, 1993, cover featuring David Letterman. On the contrary, the two-word headline, which referred to Letterman's lifelong dream to host "The Tonight Show" with the invocation, "Heeeeeeeeerrre's Dave!," resulted in humorous debate among the editors about how many *e*'s to insert in "Heeeeeeeeerrre's." Perhaps the greatest challenge, Anderson says, was persuading Letterman to pose for the Mark Seliger photograph in the first place. Letterman is said to be sensitive about his appearance, and had to be encouraged even after the pictures were shot. A Rolling Stone staffer got Letterman to autograph the cover after a taping of his show not long ago, though, "So I guess it all worked out just fine," Anderson says.

A third Rolling Stone cover that earned the judges' unanimous approval was attached not to a magazine but to a book, namely, a revised and updated edition of *The Rolling Stone Illustrated History of Rock & Roll*. "When Fred worked on that, it was our first big Adobe Illustrator

project," Anderson relates. "It was still a huge mystery to us." The ease with which Woodward could select, combine, and change colors resulted in a happy free-for-all that is now but a jaded memory as digital technology has become integrated into the life of Rolling Stone. "We were so excited that we taped together a giant color poster of the cover to show the editors at Random House. We really got into the Mac after that. That book cover sort of broke the ice."

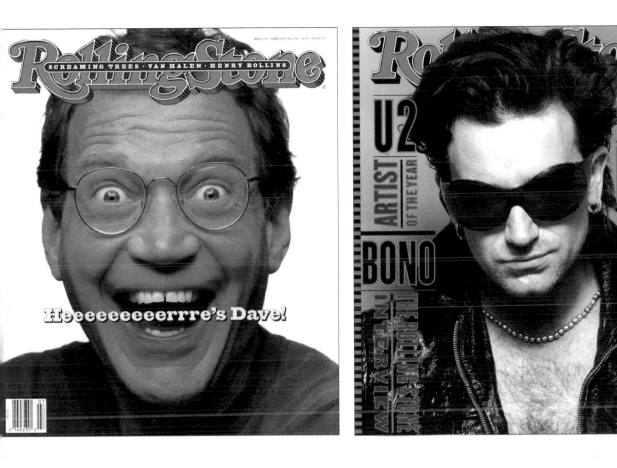

Publication: Rolling Stone, New York, NY
Art director: Fred Woodward
Photographers: Andrew MacPherson (Bono), Mark Seliger (Letterman)
Publisher (*Rolling Stone History of Rock & Roll*): Random House, New York, NY

A meandering pastoral roadside cluttered with gargantuan platters of food. Who could imagine a better way of illustrating the title *Slow Food* than to turn the sterotypical fast food landscape with its four-lane highways, smog, and golden arches, on its ear? According to Jackie Merri Meyer, art director at Warner Books, this book is for a very new niche of reader—people who love cooking and eating but don't indulge because of health reasons. "It's a cookbook and a book about the experience of food. And, yes, the art is conceptual."

Meyer designed the cover herself "not to save money"—in fact, her illustration budget was about 25 per cent more generous than usual—"but because this book was a little jewel and I knew exactly how I wanted it."

Working directly with the illustrator, Douglas Smith, she offered reference and inspiration. (Her first idea was to capture the feeling of Classico sauce labels.) "Doug likes to present more than one idea," she explains, "so when the first two roughs, which emphasized food and family, were rejected because the travel aspect of the book needed to be stronger, he worked up a new concept." Meyer selected the sketch that she thought best expressed the book's dual nature, and was delighted with the finish. "The artist did a superb job of capturing the spirit of the book. The color palette is right on."

The book sold well and has won many awards, Meyer

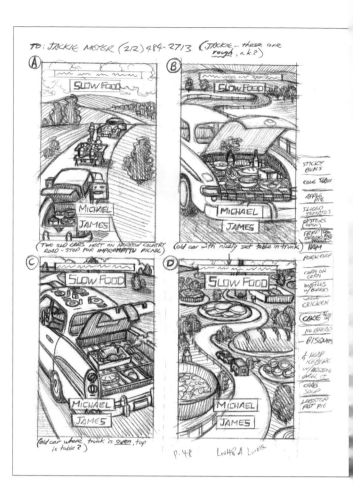

This page and opposite page, top: Douglas Smith's sketches, emphasizing travel as well as food. The lower right sketch in first image was developed into the final version; this page and opposite page, bottom: Smith's thumbnail sketches.

Flavors and Memories of America's Hometowns

SLOW FOOD

MICHAEL JAMES

reports, adding, "I'm sorry to say that the author, Michael James, did not live long enough to appreciate all the accolades."

Publisher: Warner Books, New York, NY
Art director/designer: Jackie Merri Meyer
Illustrator: Douglas Smith, Brookline, MA
Printer: Coral Graphics Services, Plainview, NY

Golden Country Jukebox Favorites

Only one day and one copyright-free postcard image from Beth Middleworth's files were required to produce this CD cover design for a compilation of country hits. Because the client, Liberty Records, didn't consider these re-released songs a major project, Middleworth, a designer with Jackson Design in Nashville, was allowed greater than usual freedom. "If a big star is involved, usually the manager, artist, and record label all have a say-so about how they think the package should look," she points out. "With a compilation, they let you come up with your own stuff and don't mess around with it too much."

Her constraints were largely imposed by the demands of the retail environment; for instance, she hand-lettered the title at a size that would be prominent in a rack display. Any typography not hand-lettered was executed in QuarkXpress. The postcard, part of Middleworth's personal collection, had been discovered in an antiques store in Kentucky.

Left: jewel box insert unfolds to reveal full length of postcard image.

Client: Liberty Records, Nashville, TN
Design firm: Jackson Design, Nashville, TN
Art director: Buddy Jackson
Designer/letterer: Beth Middleworth

When Louise Fili was assigned the cover of author William Burroughs's biography, she found the stock photographs supplied by the publisher far from inspiring. Intent on serving this unconventional writer with something unusual, she asked photographer William Duke to re-photograph and re-print a shot of Burroughs in profile— "not a great photo in and of itself, but 100 per cent better after Bill was finished with it." Fili then did a "still life," positioning plaster display letters directly on the image, which Duke photographed again. "The trickiest part," she says, "was having to use a tweezer to position $3/4''$ letters on the photograph, coping with the usual problems of alignment and letterspacing." The slightly out-of-focus effect of the typography recalls opening title sequences in industrial films from the '50s and early '60s, a nice evocation of the period when Burroughs rose to fame. And the fuzziness and shadows lend an aura of mystery to a man whose tormented life and vivid imagination seem singularly unknowable. Says Fili, "Since I do so many book jackets, I try not to repeat myself. It would have been very easy to do a straight design solution with the photograph, but I'm glad that I was able to take it a step further with the dimensional letters." The Casebook jurors agreed, making this selection a unanimous choice.

Publisher: Hyperion Books, New York, NY
Art director: Victor Weaver
Designer: Louise Fili, Louise Fili Ltd., New York, NY
Photographer: William Duke, Los Altos, CA; original photograph supplied by Bettmann Archives

The cornucopia of UCLA's offerings are presented throughout the year in thick catalogs that smell of plain, sober ink on newsprint. Nothing fancy interferes with the course descriptions, ranging from African languages to women's studies. However, alluding to this diversity in the cover design is a job that requires some creativity, and for several years it has been entrusted to a distinguished group of designers. Two recent offerings are from Paula Scher, who designed the cover of UCLA's 1992 continuing education catalog, and Paul Rand, who did the summer sessions catalog for 1993.

Working in her familiar illustration style that involves wall-to-wall handwritten copy, Scher divided a human head into sectors and labeled each with the name of a different academic discipline. "By hand-painting this quasi-phrenological chart, I put my own signature on the cover while illustrating the courses at UCLA," she explains. Presented with a series of detailed questions about the role digital technology might have played in the conception or execution of her piece, she offered the single, nonspecific word, "Never."

Rand's solution, which he tersely characterizes as "the best idea at the time," is also overwhelmingly reminiscent of its designer and equally exploits the esthetic

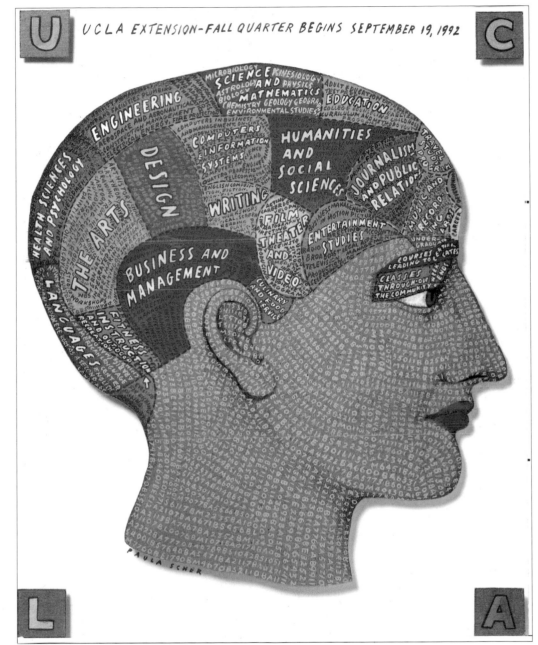

properties of letterforms. "UCLA 93" emerges in color out of a bold black alphabet, with the concept of summer expressed in a solid yellow and undeniably sunlike letter *O*. The design also appears on a poster. Both catalogs and the poster won the Casebook jury's unanimous approval.

UCLABC
DEFGHIJ
KLMNOP
QRSTUV
WXYZ93

UCLA Summer Sessions 1993

University of California, Los Angeles
Los Angeles, California 90024
March 1993

Session A: June 28–August 6
Session B: July 19–August 27
Session C: August 9–September 17

UCLA Summer Sessions 1993

University of California, Los Angeles   310 825 8355

Client: UCLA Extension, Los Angeles, CA
Creative director: InJu Sturgeon
Designers: Paula Scher, New York, NY (UCLA Extension—Fall Quarter 1992), Paul Rand, Weston, CT (UCLA Summer Sessions 1993)

Frank Baseman's poster for *Vermont Is for Lovers*, an independent movie distributed by Zeitgeist Films, conjures up the film title's kitschy nuances by incorporating familiar pop culture icons of domestic bliss: refrigerator magnets, plastic bride and groom wedding-cake figures, and the requisite "happy ending" blue sky.

Baseman elaborates: "I was supplied with a few black-and-white glossy stills from the film that were not of very good quality. I tried to work with them, but wasn't happy with the results." He felt that by using these familiar symbols instead he would come up with something that was "curious and engaging, leaving just enough to the imagination."

He was equally creative with financial considerations. "This was no large Hollywood operation, and the budget reflected that," he relates. "I decided to produce the background sky effect using a duotone of cyan and black, as opposed to full-color, so that we were not using a full-bleed color sep. After that, the largest separation was for the magnetic lettering. To save money, the letters were photographed closer in proximity to one another, and then the printer cut the film to spread them out for the poster. Finally, the whole thing was hand-stripped—a Scitex just would have been too expensive."

In fact, the whole job was pretty much hand-done. The only element of the poster composed on computer was the body copy at the top and bottom, which was made to undulate with the help of Adobe illustrator. Besides serving as a great advertisement for the film, the poster has come to be regarded as an object worth holding onto in its own right: "People have hung it in their rooms or offices long after the film has come and gone," Baseman says.

Above, left: concept sketch; above, right: color comp of Baseman's poster.

Client: Zeitgeist Films
Designer: Frank Baseman, Brooklyn, NY
Copywriters: Nancy Gerstman, Emily Russo
Photographer: Earl Ripling
Type designer: John O'Brien
Printer: JFB Litho, West Babylon, NY
Colors: 4-color process on Vintage Velvet Cover
Size: 24" by 36"

Posse

In 1993, in the wake of the L.A. riots, Frankfurt Gips Balkind decided to offer one of their summer internships to a teenager from South Central L.A. Their eventual choice was Sherwood Andrews, a senior from Crenshaw High School with a passion for drawing.

During the summer, FGB was asked to come up with a poster and collateral for the Gramercy Pictures release *Posse*, a black cowboy film primarily targeted to young black audiences and starring Mario van Peebles. Crenshaw, who was one of a number of designers working on the project, came up with the idea of presenting a pure black silhouette of a cowboy as the focal point of the poster. As he recalls, "The assignment was to think of a symbol of cowboys, and I considered a variety of shapes and objects before the silhouette crossed my mind. But once I thought of it, I knew it was the best."

Albert Watson was commissioned to photograph the actor Mario van Peebles, and designer Randi Braun devised the *P* logo—subsequently used on all other promotional materials—which mirrors the boldness and simplicity of the image.

The poster has gone on to win a key art award from The Hollywood Reporter, and Andrews, who has been the subject of a piece in the Los Angeles Times and a spot on MTV, is now a full-time FGB employee. "If I wasn't working here," Andrews claims, "I don't think I'd be able to do anything that would have to do with my interest in art."

POSSE

THIS SPRING

© Gramercy Pictures 1992

Client: Gramercy Pictures
Design firm: Frankfurt Gips Balkind, Los Angeles, CA
Creative director: Peter Bemis
Art directors: Randi Braun, Sherwood Andrews
Designer: Randi Braun
Photographer: Albert Watson
Printer: Larry Brown Litho, Los Angeles, CA
Colors: Four-color process
Size: 26 3/4" by 39 3/4"

AIGA Wichita Presents
Brad Holland

Although New York illustrator Brad Holland and Atlanta designer Jim McCune have met only once, they have managed, through faxes and Fed Ex, to create over a dozen posters together over the years. Their most recent collaborative effort was this one announcing a speaking engagement by Holland at the Wichita Chapter of the American Institute of Graphic Arts.

Holland's painting had originally been done for an article about healthcare in Mother Jones magazine, and he was so pleased with it that he decided to use it again for the Wichita piece: "I thought a poster would be a way to extend and prolong the picture's life." AIGA Wichita Chapter president Sonia Greteman, who coordinated the production for the poster, was extremely pleased with the results: "We broke all attendance records at the event, and it's still hanging all over town in designer's offices."

Everyone agreed that the effect of the poster would be ruined if it was folded up as a mailer, so McCune and Greteman decided to pick up a detail from the painting and produce it off the same press run with an identical type treatment. Holland didn't see it until reaching Wichita, but was "delighted" when he did.

Says McCune, "I always keep in mind what the posters are for and let Brad's work do the talking. I avoid design trends and decorations and anything else that would get in the way of his image. Brad's a pleasure to work with." Holland adds, "A lot of designers think a design has to prove something. Jim understands that good design is less about making impressive decisions than about making right ones."

Clients: AIGA Wichita (KS) Chapter, Brad Holland
Art directors: Brad Holland, Sonia Greteman
Designer: Jim McCune/Communicorp Inc., Atlanta, GA
Illustrator/letterer: Brad Holland
Printer: Donlevy Lithograph, Wichita, KS
Colors: 4-color process
Size: 19 3/4" by 23 3/4"

Right: mailer for the event printed off the same press run with a detail from Holland's painting.

Expressing the vitality of jazz in visual form has long been a favorite theme of visual artists, and it was certainly the motivation for Andy Cruz, of Brand Design in Wilmington, when he began working on this poster for a jazz series: "The free-flowing brushstrokes parallel the nuances of jazz music. We wanted to project it as an art form and appeal to a wide range of people in the surrounding region."

The client, The Interneighborhood Foundation, is a small not-for-profit agency, with few funds for promotional materials. Cruz decided the best bet was to reflect "the artistic simplicity of jazz music" with a parallel simplicity of both form and materials. Because the poster had to be fairly large, the budget limited Cruz to the use of two colors and a relatively inexpensive stock. After the piece was printed, however, he was not happy with the heaviness of either color, and he persuaded the printer to run the posters through for a second pass, resulting in a stronger graphic statement. "It became extremely popular—we often receive requests for copies even though the series is over," Cruz reports. "Also, attendance for the series increased by over 75 per cent."

Client: The Interneighborhood Foundation
Design firm: Brand Design Co., Wilmington, DE
Designer: Andy Cruz
Printer: Henry Grabowski/Diamond Printing Co.
Colors: Black and opaque white on Riegel PCW Cover, Chino
Size: 17 3/4" by 34 3/4"

Right: Cruz's preliminary sketches for the final poster.

Tom Schifanella, an art director at Robin Shepherd studios in Jacksonville, Florida, has learned not to bark at clients who like to offer creative input. When Charlotte Mabrey and Bob White of the University of North Florida music department hired the firm several years ago to design a poster for their first annual contemporary music and performance event, they had one suggestion for an identity: a dog.

"The poster has become the perfect vehicle to illustrate the concerts," Schifanella states. "They always combine performance art and music, and we've used the dog in various visual ways to suggest this combination." After working through a series of ideas about how to treat the pooch for the 1992 poster (the fifth in the series), designer and client finally decided on this depiction of an ultra-hip canine with cool shades. "The audience is college students," Schifanella explains, "so I usually try to use a powerful visual, minimal copy, and very contemporary color combinations to catch their eye." A sure sign of continued success is the high incidence of student theft (as with other college posters in this volume): "Most are usually stolen immediately after the concert and put up in dorm rooms around campus."

To save on costs—the budget for this year's poster was $500 for design, production, and printing—Schifanella has chosen silkscreen as a printing process (with handmixed colors), and always tries to keep the edition size below 100. "In some cases, we have had specific requests for posters from people attending the concert," he says, "and we've been able to reprint small editions for sale."

Left and above left: Schifanella's other concept sketches for the poster.

Client: University of North Florida Music Department, Jacksonville, FL
Design firm: Robin Shepherd Studios, Jacksonville, FL
Art director/copywriter/illustrator: Tom Schifanella
Printer: Cox Fine Art, Jacksonville, FL
Color: Four hand-mixed colors on Simpson Evergreen
Size: 24" by 36"

Leonard J. Waxdeck's 29th Annual
Bird Calling Contest

David Bartels, principal of the St. Louis–based Bartles, Carstens & Associates, is no stranger to Leonard J. Waxdeck's Bird Calling Contest. In fact, this is the 10th poster he's created for the event (see PRINT Casebook 8), which takes place each year at Piedmont High School in Piedmont, California, where the eponymous Waxdeck teaches biology. The contest involves 40 finalists (all from the high school's student population) performing their best bird calls in front of students, guests, and a panel of judges, and has gained a nationwide following with repeated appearances by finalists on "The Tonight Show" as well as other TV venues.

Bartels's original reasons for offering to design a pro bono poster for the event remain the same today: "It helps make kids well-rounded, and the subject is visually rich." The 1992 poster varies a bit from earlier ones in its utilization of photography as opposed to illustration. As Bartels relates, "The photo [by Dallas-based Tom Ryan] was originally done as a photographer's sample. We really liked the power of the image, and this was a nice way of keeping the series fresh."

The photo is complimented with lively calligraphy by designer Brian Barclay. "It was our desire to create a type design that was lyrical in feel, with a primitive quality to it," Bartels explains. "The type was grayed back so it became a part of the background, allowing the figure to remain dominant."

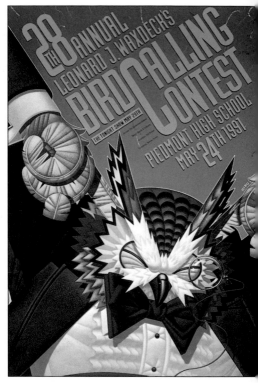

This page: posters from past years. Opposite page: The 1992 poster is the first in the series to utilize photography instead of illustration.

Client: Leonard J. Waxdeck Bird-Calling Contest, Piedmont High School, Piedmont, CA
Design firm: Bartels, Carstens & Associates, St. Louis, MO
Art director: David Bartels
Designer: Tom Ryan
Printer: Ultra Color, St. Louis, MO
Color: Black
Size: 26 1/2" by 17 3/8"

In July 1992, YA-I Amanda Chen was asked to design a poster for an exhibition of 20th-century furniture in Taiwan, where she was living at the time. The result was a poster design with a truly symbiotic relationship with its subject matter.

A majority of the chairs which make up the outline of a human torso in the poster are landmarks of Modern design, and the form=function equation of that school is echoed by Chen in her conception, as well as execution, of the piece. As she states, "I wanted to realize the functional nature of the chair, while retaining a sense of humor about what is 'natural.'"

The designer was pleased with the results, citing favorable reactions from exhibition visitors ("people especially loved the central chair") as well as an overall sense of satisfaction with her solution: "These are timeless icons of 20th-century design, and I think the poster design is timeless as well."

In fact, when Chen moved to the U.S. last year to start a graduate design degree, she decided to produce the poster again as a self-promotion piece. "The black-and-white format is easy to reproduce with different copy, and I'm hoping the poster can be used again here for future furniture exhibitions."

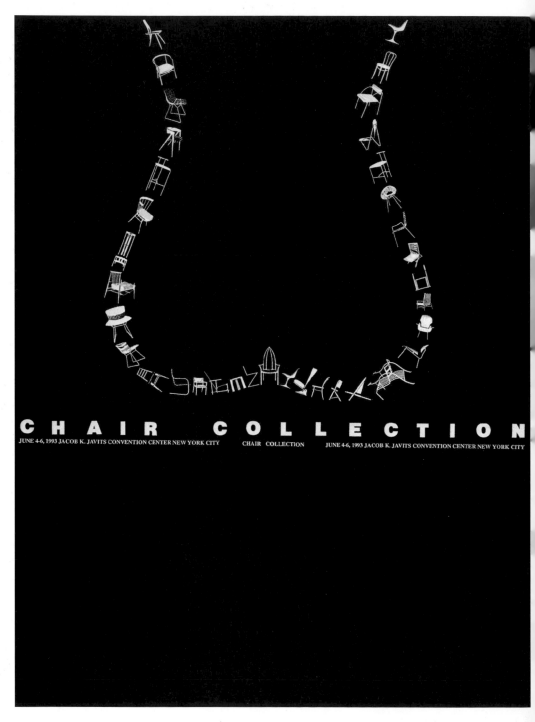

Client: A.C. Associates, Chatham, NJ
Design firm: A.C. Associates
Art director/copywriter: YA-I Amanda Chen
Photographer: Mahmut Gunes
Printer: SoHo Service, New York, NY
Colors: White on Simpson matte black
Size: 20" by 30"

Culture Clash

The San Francisco Museum of Modern Art's Design Lecture series promises "lively conversation," and art director Margaret Youngblood decided it was important to take this into account when she was asked by the San Francisco AIGA to put together a poster for the 1992 event. "We wanted to suggest to the public that the speakers, with their varying backgrounds, might support different points of view," explains Youngblood. With speakers running the gamut from Gianni Versace to Paul Rand to Maira Kalman, such a strategy was well advised.

Originally, Youngblood and designer Doug Becker planned to use a Xeroxed photo of Kalman in the poster design: "It was much more powerful, in my opinion," Youngblood opines. However, in deference to the other four speakers, they chose instead an image by photographer Kevin Ng. The poster, created in a silkscreen edition of 30 for bus shelters, and in a smaller-sized edition of 500, was designed traditionally, with Xeroxes and markers, and was created with the context in mind. As Youngblood relates, "Bus shelters are big; we wanted the faces to be bigger than life."

The computer was only brought into play afterward, when the photos were scanned in on Photoshop to create a coarser pattern. The art was subsequently generated in Illustrator on a Macintosh FX. The designers had to limit their palette to two colors due to a limited budget. Budget, however, was the only limitation they had to face. The arrangement the museum has with the AIGA is such that designers are given total control over the project. As Youngblood puts it, "They got what we gave them."

The final product was a big hit, especially in bus shelters. "If a poster is nice, Gannett will leave it up for a while," she says. "Some of these can still be found in the city."

Client: San Francisco Museum of Modern Art
Design firm: Landor Associates, San Francisco, CA
Art director: Margaret Youngblood
Designers: Margaret Youngblood, Doug Becker
Photographer: Kevin Ng
Illustrator/production: Bruce McCoovert
Printer: JOMAC, Oakland, CA
Colors: Black and red
Size: 4' by 6'

Catherine the Great

When Champion International developed new hues for their Carnival line of colored papers, they asked Pentagram designer Susan Hochbaum to select illustrators to create a series of promotional posters on the mill's paper. The new colors were dubbed "Carnival Royals," and it was decided that the series would have the theme of "Royal Follies."

As Hochbaum relates, "Research turned up a wealth of information on the eccentricities of royal family members; Napoleon, Catherine the Great, Louis XIV and others provided enough extraordinary behavior to inspire the whole project." Hochbaum chose illustrator Jeffrey Fisher to evince the Russian monarch's rather paranoid response to her baldness: Apparently, Catherine was so concerned with her secret being kept that she locked up her hairdresser in an iron cage for three years to prevent him from spreading gossip about her wig.

Fisher's solution displays his characteristic whimsy and invention, and as Hochbaum relates, perfectly fulfills the requirements of the client: "The production challenge for the project was to find a way to demonstrate these papers' printability. We wanted to suggest to designers, who were the primary audience, alternate ways of getting strong color on darker paper, and Jeffrey's piece managed to do so in a engaging way."

The poster, like all of the others in the series, was silkscreened in three colors, and was "snapped off Champion's sample table," according to Hochbaum, at the 1991 AIGA conference.

Catherine the Great

The Russian Empress Catherine the Great (1760-1796) was so ashamed of her baldness that she locked up her hairdresser in an iron cage for three years so he wouldn't gossip about the wig she wore. The current popular assumption is that Great Catherine wore a blond wig because of the Marlene Dietrich film, but all of her wigs were definitely Royal Black.

Carnival Royal from Champion

Client: Champion International Corp., Stamford, CT
Design firm: Pentagram, New York, NY
Designer: Susan Hochbaum
Illustrator: Jeffrey Fisher
Printer: Ambassador Arts, New York, NY
Colors: Three colors silkscreened on Carnival Royal 80-lb. black
Size: 24" by 37"

The Big Apple Festival

Every autumn, downtown Manhattan, regarded by many as the nerve center of the world's financial and business interests, kicks off its wingtips and goes a little bit country. The event in question is the Big Apple Festival, a "country fair" held each year at the World Financial Center in Battery Park City.

Kent Hunter, of New York's Frankfurt Balkind Partners, was interested in conveying the mood of the event to New Yorkers when asked to design this poster for the 1992 festival. "The poster was intended to attract families to the event, which consists of pig races, apple cider, music, and the like," Hunter explains. "I wanted to use a folk art 'naive' style, hand-painted lettering, and bright, happy colors."

Hunter had just the right illustrator in mind for the job: "I've wanted to find just the right project for Laura Levine for a long time, and this poster proved perfect," he recalls, adding, "We share a passion for folk art and had lots of fun collaborating." Levine was pleased that he thought of her for a project that was so well suited to her interests and style. "It fell together really quickly," she remarks, adding, "It was my first poster, and it was really exciting to walk around and see it sniped all over town."

Clients: Battery Park City Authority, Olympia and York Arts and Events, New York, NY
Design firm: Frankfurt Balkind Partners, New York, NY
Art director: Kent Hunter
Illustrator: Laura Levine
Hand letterers: Laura Levine, Kent Hunter
Printer: Walbern Press, New York, NY
Colors: 4-color process on S.D. Warren Patina 80-lb. Text
Size: 26" by 38"

Playboy of the West Indies

This poster is just one of 15 illustrator Jim McMullan has created for New York City's Lincoln Center (others include his much-acclaimed poster for John Guare's *Six Degrees of Separation*).

As with the previous posters, McMullan followed a certain routine: "I had meetings with the director, the artistic director, and the executive producer, who gave me their views on Mustapha Matura's play. In addition, I was given a video of a previous production. I also discussed how the play was seen in marketing terms with Jim Russek, whose advertising agency was responsible for marketing it."

The play is actually based on John Millington Synge's *Playboy of the Western World* (1905), in which a charismatic young man returns to the Irish fishing village of his youth. The villagers welcome him with open arms, perceiving him as a glamorous, appealing figure until his father, whom he thinks he killed but actually only wounded before he left, returns to confront him. The villagers subsequently turn on the protagonist, and the play ends with his accusing them of hypocrisy.

Playboy of the West Indies changes the location from Ireland to the Caribbean. "One of the major characteristics of the original play was its heavy reliance on Irish brogue, and Matura felt that the Trinidadian patois was just as rich," McMullan explains.

In a sense, the very theme of the play, namely, the ways in which people's perceptions are shaped, also informed the treatment of the poster. His first sketch was deemed "too serious" by his clients, who were concerned that the farcical nature of the play would be misrepresented, even though its subject matter is ultimately quite serious. "Despite the fact that he actually arrives on the scene in a hangdog state," McMullan says, "I made the gesture of the protagonist more exuberant." The final image, which evokes the sensual languor of the tropics, appeared as a three-sheet poster around Lincoln Center as well as a windowcard in ticket offices.

Client: Lincoln Center Theater, New York, NY
Design firm: James McMullan Inc., New York, NY
Agency: Russek Advertising, New York, NY
Art director: Jim Russek
Illustrator: James McMullan
Printer: Verillen Graphics, Brookfield, CT
Colors: 4-color process on 80-lb. coated white
Size: 30" by 46" and 14" by 22" theater lobby card

Above: preliminary sketches made before and after taking the reference photo (opposite page).

It seems the best way to get students at Brigham Young University in Provo, Utah, to register for the winter semester is to focus their interest on the activities that are probably responsible for their inattention: winter sports.

Designer McRay Magleby took this into account when creating these two posters for BYU, enhancing their appeal with stark, dramatic illustrations, which happened to be two of 13 images commissioned from the designer for Salt Lake City's bid book for the 1998 Winter Olympics. "The art director for the Olympics project, Adrian Pulfer, asked me to do something with a woodcut feel," Magleby recalls. "But we weren't happy with the antiquated look, so I decided to update their appearance by making the images more streamlined."

For the BYU posters, the designer chose the black-and-white illustrations he had for two of the events—skiing and skating—then added color and a silver trap line. They are literally underlined with a simple type treatment, with each line of sans-serif upper-case text reducing in size, emphasizing the idea of time running out. When asked why he chose the rich magenta and blue colors for the posters, Magleby responds, somewhat sheepishly, "Well, they're the colors of my ski parka."

Client: Brigham Young University, Provo, UT
Design firm: BYU Graphics
Art director: McRay Magleby
Designers/illustrators: McRay Magleby, David Eliason
Copywriter: Norman Darais
Type designer: Jonathan Skousan
Printer: Rory Robinson
Colors: Blue, magenta, and black on Karma White 80-lb. cover
Size: 26" by 40"

In the early fall of 1991, Designing New York, an ad hoc group of designers and architects, sponsored a colloquium on ways to improve the quality of life in New York City. Michael Bierut, a member of the executive committee and a partner at Pentagram, was asked to design an invitation and poster for the event.

He based the poster design on an image he had originally created for the group's letterhead, and when asked how he came up with this solution, Bierut deadpanned, "I really don't know—I'm usually more articulate about these things." With a little prodding, he began offering interpretations like, "The black represents the vastness of the celestial void," and "the progressively smaller type represents a dwindling cry against the dark night." Allowing for Bierut's well-known pranksterish wit, his initial response will be familiar to any designer who's happened to come up with a solution that's just right, even if he's not absolutely sure why.

"It's not a very hardworking poster," he adds, noting that it wasn't used as a mailer, and was actually only distributed by hand, "but I'm happy with the results." The design was regenerated again by Bierut for a poster announcing a series of "charettes"—workshops on specific areas of urban life like the subway and city parks—that featured the original design overlaid with elements of color referring to the topics under consideration.

Below: Bierut's preliminary sketch; cover of invitation to breakfast debate held during the symposium.

Client: Designing New York Committee, New York, NY
Design firm: Pentagram, New York, NY
Designer/copywriter: Michael Bierut
Printer: Ambassador Arts, New York, NY
Colors: 4-color process
Size: 24" by 36"

1993 Nuclear Plant Experience Conference

Every year and a half, the Nuclear Plant Experience Conference (NPEC) takes place in historic Williamsburg, Virginia. For the 1993 event, designer/illustrator Michael Schwab was retained to create a conference poster that would present a "positive, healthy image" of the meeting's subject as well as tie it to the colonial environment that served as backdrop.

Schwab, well-known for his nostalgic illustration style, worked from a series of snapshots taken of a Williamsburg blacksmith to devise an image that reflected the conference theme, "Forging Our Industry's Future." The "historic" effect was enhanced by other elements, such as the use of an antique serif typeface presented in declining point size (a common conceit of newspaper layouts in the 1800s), the vertically oriented proportions (reminiscent of posters from the colonial era), and hand-produced screen printing on a Speckletone stock.

Schwab's original treatment showed a stylized figure shaping the image of the atom on an anvil. The client, B&W Nuclear Technologies, preferred an alternative configuration. "It was agreed that he should be 'admiring' it rather than hammering it," Schwab says. Larry Bevins, whose firm Imagination by Design in Lynchburg, Virginia, coordinated the project, was impressed with the level of communication between client and designer: "The client was very good at articulating what was wanted and needed, and Michael was super in translating these wishes into something that was both appropriate and esthetic."

Below: reference photo; first preliminary sketch for poster.

Client: B&W Nuclear Technologies, Lynchburg, VA
Design firms: Michael Schwab Design, San Francisco, CA and Imagination by Design, Lynchburg, VA
Art directors: Larry Bevins, Richard Gentile, Bill Warner
Designer/illustrator: Michael Schwab
Copywriter: Richard Gentile
Printer: Overington Graphics, Roanoke, VA
Colors: Six colors on French Speckletone recycled stock
Size: 21" by 36"

Juilliard IV, Cubist Cello

Designer Milton Glaser had one goal in mind when he was asked to do a poster (his fifth) for New York City's renowned Juilliard School: "I wanted to suggest that Juilliard was a creative and lively place," the designer relates. Working with a long deadline and a generous budget, Glaser decided to look at several of Picasso's collages based around musical themes, and then transfer and transform the Cubist sensibility into a solution. The resulting poster is a masterly mix of colors and patterns that evoke both the vibrancy of musical expression and the school's stature.

Interestingly, a Juilliard representative expressed some concern about the poster's image of a dissected cello, worrying that literal-minded musicians might read it as destructive, but that opinion was overridden, and the piece was produced as submitted by Glaser. It was then placed at various locations around Lincoln Center (where the school is located), as well as high schools and other places where students and parents might see it. Glaser was pleased with the positive reception accorded the design, and notes that it is still being used by the school.

Client: The Juilliard School, New York
Design firm: Milton Glaser Inc.
Designer: Milton Glaser
Printer: Brodock Press, Utica, NY
Colors: 4-color process
Size: 24" by 36"

Blue Corn

When The Body Shop, the environmentally conscious cosmetics chain, began manufacturing a line of products made from blue corn, company founder and president Anita Roddick decided to focus the product promotion on the indigenous culture of the Santa Pueblo region in New Mexico, where large quantities of the crop are harvested. Paul Davis was approached by art director Eric Baker to illustrate a large poster to be displayed in the chain's stores.

As Davis recalls, "We had enough time to do detailed research at the National Museum of the American Indian, where we had access to extensive archives of vintage photographs." From those, Davis did a preliminary sketch of a young Native American girl in traditional garb and hairstyle carrying several ears of blue corn in a tray, set against an arid landscape with a yellow sky.

The finished poster is similar except for a few minor compositional changes—for example, the tray is gone and the girl cradles the corn in her arms. Davis claims his goal is "to create drama" in his theater posters, and in this case he certainly succeeded: The poster has been featured in international exhibitions and has won several awards.

Below: Davis's first preliminary sketch.

Client: The Body Shop
Design firm: Eric Baker Design Associates, New York
Art director: Eric Baker
Illustrator/hand letterer: Paul Davis
Printer: Kenner Printing Co., New York, NY
Colors: 4-color process
Size: 40 ½" by 59"

Some time ago, an agreement was reached at Pentagram Design regarding pro bono speaking engagements. As Kit Hinrichs relates, "Several of my partners and I decided that, in exchange for the time given to prepare and deliver a speech, we were allowed to design the poster. This has led to better-attended speeches and posters that we don't have to hide in drawers."

Hinrichs came up with the design of this poster promoting his speaking tour through Australia while glancing around his San Francisco office. Among other items was a prop from a previous photo shoot: an ANZAC (Australian and New Zealand Army Corps) hat. "I wanted to convey something about myself to the people I would be meeting, as well as using imagery that would be representative of their country," Hinrichs says. "The flag was appropriate in two ways: I'm an American, and I'm also an ardent flag collector." Enlarging the hat was a whimsical touch that happened to allude to Australia's vastness—"It just seemed right," he asserts.

When Hinrichs was asked some time later to speak at the Dallas Society of Visual Communications, he decided to retain the imagery, with minor modifications. As he recalls, "The idea of building on an existing theme seemed interesting—a Stetson just seemed more appropriate for the speech in Texas."

HINRICHS

IN DALLAS

The posters were designed, typeset, and composed on QuarkXPress, and in both cases, a disk with accompanying transparencies was sent to the host organization for production. Hinrichs plans to continue using the "big hat, little Kit" theme for future speaking engagements, providing he can include elements that successfully reference the host organization's environs.

Meanwhile, back in San Francisco, the response has been enthusiastic. A staff member at the Pentagram office recently affixed a note to the Hinrichs-in-Australia poster with the following notation: "Honey, I Shrunk the Kit!"

Hinrichs in Australia
Client: Spicers Paper Ltd., Pretoria, Australia
Design firm: Pentagram, San Francisco, CA
Designer: Kit Hinrichs
Computer artist: Shelly Reilly
Photographer: Bob Esparza, San Francisco, CA
Copywriter: Dalphine Hirasuna/ Hirasuna Editorial Services, San Francisco, CA
Printing: Canberra Press, Mordialloc, Australia
Colors: 4-color process on Volare plus 150 GSM
Size: 24" by 34"

Hinrichs in Dallas
Client: Dallas Society of Visual Communications, Dallas, TX
Design firm: Pentagram, San Francisco, CA
Designer: Kit Hinrichs
Computer artist: Erich Schreck
Photographer: Bob Esparza, San Francisco, CA
Copywriter: Dalphine Hirasuna/ Hirasuna Editorial Services, San Francisco, CA
Printing: Heritage Press, Dallas, TX
Colors: 4-color process on Simpson Equinox Lunar Ivory 70 lb. Text
Size: 17" by 24"

Every once in a while, a
designer comes up with a
solution so simple that it
seems to lack any design at
all. When the Dallas Society of
Visual Communications
invited Paula Scher to give a
lecture in September 1992,
the designer was also asked to
create a poster announcing
the engagement that would be
sent to all members of the
organization and other
potential attendees.

    Because this was, in
Scher's words, "a design for
designers," and because she
needed to do it "fast and
cheap," she came up with
a design stripped down to
the bare minimum: By
manipulating the space within
the big *D* (i.e., Dallas) to
conform to the outline of a
"skinny *P*" (for Paula, as in the
diminutive Scher), she
distilled the particulars of the
speaking engagement down
to their bare essence. Body
copy was then run in the
space of the *P*. This purely
typographic solution, created
entirely on computer, was a
big hit in Dallas. "Everyone
said it was stunning," Scher
recalls, and adds, almost as an
afterthought, "I think it was
stunning, too."

Client: Dallas Society of Visual
Communications
Design firm: Pentagram, New York,
NY
Art director/copywriter: Paula Scher
Designers: Paula Scher, Ron Louie
Printer: The Graphics Group, Dallas,
TX
Colors: 4-color process
Size: 16 1/2" by 23 1/4"

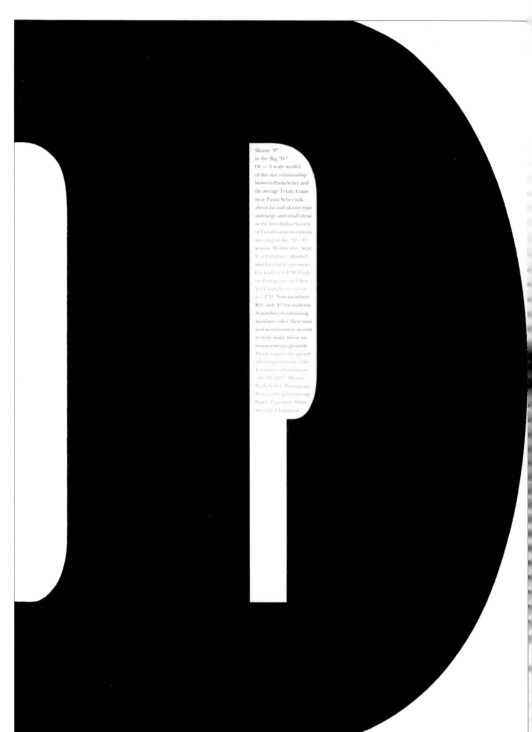

Twenty-One Years of Design in Japan

Kenneth Grange, a partner at Pentagram in London, gave a lecture in 1992 at London's Royal Society of Arts on the products he had designed for various Japanese companies. Woody Pirtle, a Pentagram partner in New York, was asked to come up with a poster for the speaking engagement.

"The inspiration was the Japanese flag," Pirtle relates. "Kenneth supplied images of his product designs, and then the poster was implemented by my design team from one of my rough thumbnail sketches." In this case, Pirtle felt that size was extremely important: "I wanted the poster to be as large as possible to approach the actual size of a flag."

Because the poster was silkscreened, a whole other set of concerns had to be addressed in its production. As Pirtle explains, "Because we utilized halftones, there were critical considerations with regard to the number of dots-per-inch or line screen." A one-color treatment was not only necessary from a budgetary standpoint, but also perfectly appropriate to the poster's esthetic. Pirtle was pleased with the results: "It communicated the most important theme—Kenneth Grange's work in Japan—in a visually succinct way."

Client: Royal Society of Arts, London, UK
Design firm: Pentagram, New York, NY
Designer: Woody Pirtle
Color: Red
Size: 47" by 33"

While on a visiting professorship at the Nova Scotia College of Art and Design at the beginning of 1992, designer Gad Almaliah came across a number of Israeli posters in the school's archives. "It just so happened that we had this big collection at our disposal, and I decided to initiate a retrospective exhibition," Almaliah says. His interest was at least partly personal: He had only recently moved from Tel Aviv to start up a design practice in Boston.

As organizer of the exhibition, he was also responsible for designing a poster for the event. "It was obviously designed for Canadians, who recognize the intended combination of the two national symbols," Almaliah relates. The show has since traveled to New York City's School of Visual Arts, and Almaliah's poster for that show featured a similar juxtaposition: "For that one, I replaced the maple leaf with the Manhattan skyline," he reports.

Client: The Nova Scotia College of Art and Design, Halifax, Nova Scotia, Canada
Design firm: The Design Lab, Boston, MA
Designer: Gad Almaliah
Photographer: Brian Thompson, Medicine Hat, Alberta, Canada
Printer: Achdut, Tel Aviv, Israel
Colors: 4-color process on white Chromalux
Size: 16 3/4" by 27 3/4"

Medicine Hat
Cultural Centre Gallery
Medicine Hat, AB.

Atlantic Jewish
Council

With Co-operation of
The Canadian Hadassah-Wizo
Women's Organization

Israel in poster design

An exhibition of Israeli poster design of the last 43 years, on cultural, social and commercial subjects.

September 1 to October 1, 1992
Medicine Hat Cultural Centre Gallery
Weekdays open 10 a.m. to 8 p.m. and
Weekends from 1 p.m. to 4 p.m.
Curated By Gad Almaliah
Closing reception - October 1, 8 p.m. with
Israeli designer, Gad Almaliah in attendance

Design: Gad Almaliah
Printing: Achdut Printing Tel Aviv
Separations: Reprovize Ltd.
Plates: Phelho Ltd.
Photography: Brian Thompson
Typography: Total Graphics

In this self-published poster by Israeli artist/designer Dan Reisinger, two of the century's most potent political symbols—the red star of the U.S.S.R. and the swastika of Nazi Germany—are combined to create a powerful statement about the emergence of nationalism and fascism in the splintered territories of the former Soviet Union.

Reisinger has produced other posters with relevant political themes (such as one on Chernobyl in 1986 and another on the Gulf War in 1991). He sees them as "personal statements, which I publish from time to time in poster form." Each is mailed to the Israeli press and members of Parliament, as well as sold as a limited edition. This most recent poster was cited by the chairman of the Israeli Parliament, and was also published and discussed in the Israeli press.

The power of the piece lies in its utter simplicity. As Reisinger relates, "No preliminary sketches were made. The star was cut out in its geometric shape on red paper, then torn freely. The torn parts were then positioned and pasted on the black background." The tag line, "AGAIN?," was designed on the Mac, and then printed in white by Omnichrome on transparent film for positioning.

Despite the universal significance of the two symbols, and the obvious clarity of the final product, Reisinger was interested to find that "some people in Israel confused the five-pointed red star with the six-pointed Star of David, thereby missing the transnational message." The poster also garnered quite a bit of praise from Reisinger's peers. He received letters of admiration from Paul Rand, Fukuda, Ben Bos, and Uwe Loesch, among others.

Client: Studio Reisinger, Tel Aviv, Israel
Design firm: Studio Reisinger
Designer: Dan Reisinger
Copy: Studio Reisinger
Printer: Omanut Hadfus, Tel Aviv, Israel
Colors: Warm red and black
Size: 39 3/8" by 27 1/2"

Sometimes, a design firm's toughest client happens to be the design firm itself. Such was the case when Minneapolis-based Gardner Design decided to produce a poster celebrating its 10th anniversary (it would also double as a party invitation). As principal Nancy Gardner remembers, "Since it was for the firm, we wanted to strike a balance between designing something creative and attention-getting and something inexpensive to produce. We agonized over many designs before arriving at the final one."

The result is the essence of economy, in terms of both esthetics and budget. "We wanted a strong graphic that was a clean, humorous, and unique representation of our firm. By adding the crayon and handwriting the *O,* we made each poster unique." The piece was printed in one color, with the black being double-hit and then covered with varnish for increased depth of coverage.

The real challenge came when the sheets arrived from the printer. As Gardner recalls, "We had a four-person assembly line: one hot-glued the crayon, one drew the *O,* and two people rolled, inserted, labeled, and stamped the poster and tube." The poster—and the party—was a big success. "We found large inflatable crayons to direct guests to our new office space, and the party was very well-attended," Gardner says, adding, "Only three people wanted different colored crayons."

Client/design firm: Gardner Design, Minneapolis, MN
Art director: Nancy Gardner
Designer: Brian Collins
Illustrators: Joel Templin, Brian Collins
Copywriter: Chuck Carlson

Letterer: Yas Bakshian
Printer: Co-Op Printing, Minneapolis, MN
Colors: Black on Cross Pointe Torchglow Opaque Colonial White, 50-lb. smooth.
Size: 22" by 32"

Frankie and Johnny in the Clair de Lune

The plot of this Terence McNally play revolves around the romance between a short-order cook and a waitress in a greasy-spoon diner. When Peter Good was asked to design a poster for a production of the play in Hartford, he decided to depend on a rendering of objects as opposed to the characters themselves to evoke the play's ambience.

"The drawing has a fresh, unstylized quality which was appropriate to the play's sensibilities, and the illicit relationship between utensils adds humor," Good says. He used a Mac to generate the sans-serif type headlines and body copy, as well as the precise blocks of color. Both elements form a suitable counterbalance to the loose, almost cartoonish drawing, giving the play its own identity while reinforcing the presence of the theater itself.

Good notes a generally enthusiastic response, and expresses satisfaction with the job: "I feel the poster reflected the nature of the theater company as well as the specific play."

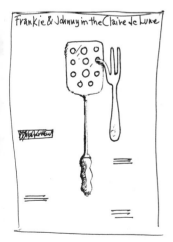

Above and right: preliminary sketches for the final poster.

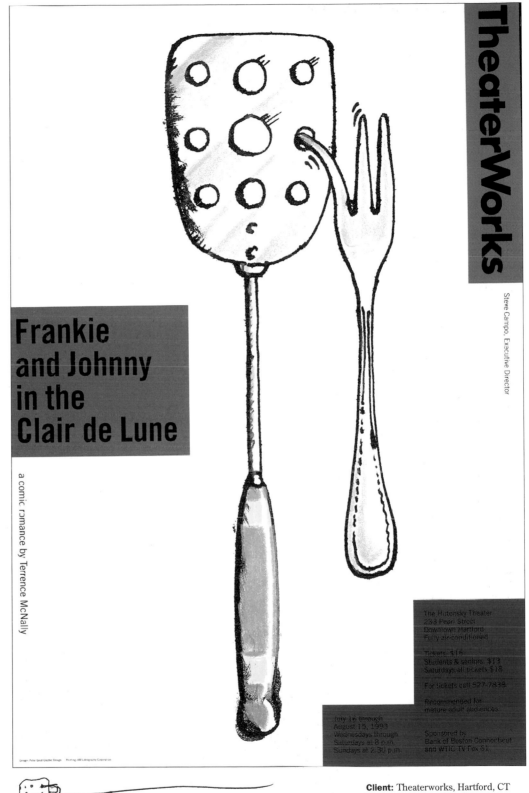

TheaterWorks

Steve Campo, Executive Director

Frankie and Johnny in the Clair de Lune

a comic romance by Terence McNally

The Hutensky Theater
233 Pearl Street
Downtown Hartford
Fully air-conditioned

Tickets: $16
Students & seniors: $13
Saturdays all tickets $18

For tickets call 527-7838

Recommended for mature adult audiences.

July 16 through
August 15, 1993
Wednesdays through
Saturdays at 8 p.m.
Sundays at 2:30 p.m.

Sponsored by
Bank of Boston Connecticut
and WTIC TV Fox 61

Design: Peter Good Graphic Design   Printing: AM Lithography Corporation

Client: Theaterworks, Hartford, CT
Design firm: Peter Good Graphic Design, Chester, CT
Designer/Illustrator: Peter Good
Copywriter: Steve Campo
Printer: AM Lithography Corp., Chicopee, MA (pro bono)
Colors: 4-color process on Quintessence Dull Cover, 80-lb. white
Size: 24" by 36"

Both Vittorio Costarella and Robynne Raye, who are partners at the Seattle studio Modern Dog, know the value of a good poster in a large urban environment. "Because Seattle is a major poster town, it's our job to design posters that jump off the wall," Costarella asserts. And like that firm's many other effective designs for the Seattle Repertory Theatre, these two offerings combine simplicity with invention to produce an effective solution.

Costarella was responsible for the poster announcing a staging of George Bernard Shaw's *Heartbreak House*. "The play features a house shaped by the characters under its roof," he explains. "At first, I used Illustrator to lay out the type, but it looked like a tract house in the suburbs. 'Heartbreak House' was a country house full of character and characters, so it needed to be shaped by hand. I took the computer type and manipulated it with Omnichrome, a heat transfer, until it took shape on its own." He adds, jokingly, "I just couldn't live in a tract house and be happy."

Costarella credits Seattle Rep associate art director Douglas Hughes with being flexible when it came to changing the initial solution: "He was kind enough and smart enough to accept the change as a much better way to go."

Says Costarella, "When I spray-mounted the Omnichrome to a colored stock, it produced a subtle third color. Our screenprinters were able to reproduce the effect by manipulating one of the screens—so, in effect, only

Below, left to right: final art as it was output from computer, and two trial versions manipulated with Omnichrome.

two screens were used to attain the weathered look."

In the end, Costarella was extremely pleased with the results—"It's one of my personal favorites," he claims—and feels the poster did what he had set out to accomplish: "The poster's shape and type treatment really 'popped.'"

A similar ingenuity can be seen in Robynne Raye's poster for a production of Jon Robin Baitz's *The Substance of Fire*. "I always try to capture some part of the play," she explains. "In a pivotal moment, the father of a failing publishing company literally burns a part of his past. The fire was a very purifying act. Also, there was an underlying theme about censorship and the fire happened to tie in nicely with that.

"It only took about five minutes to design in PageMaker, since I knew exactly how it should look," she continues, "but the burning took another five hours." Raye enlisted the promotions director at the Rep and a friend to "torch" each of the 400 posters. Because the main visual element was the pattern of burns, every poster ended up with a unique appearance. "The best compliment came after I attended the play and overhead an elderly gentleman comment to his partner, 'Did you see the poster? I think someone burned them!'" Raye recalls.

"I'm so used to designing with 'no budget' that it's instinctual," she says. "The final cost for 400 posters on recycled paper came in at $360; I spent an extra $15 on Butane and a torch."

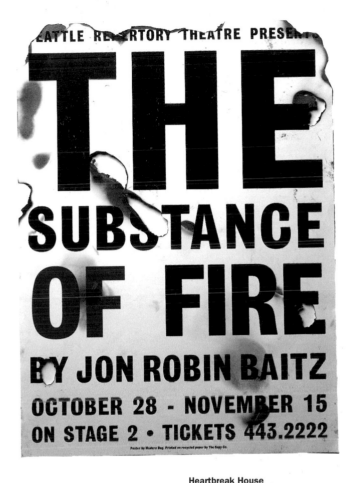

Below: small-space ad in which burn marks are approximated with a halftone screen.

Heartbreak House
Client: Seattle Repertory Theatre
Design firm: Modern Dog, Seattle, WA
Art directors: Vittorio Costarella, Douglas Hughes
Designer: Vittorio Costarella
Printer: Two-Dimensions, Seattle, WA
Colors: PMS 195, 156, 484 on Simpson Ecopaque
Size: 22" by 24"

The Substance of Fire
Client: Seattle Repertory Theatre
Design firm: Modern Dog, Seattle, WA
Art directors: Robynne Raye, Douglas Hughes
Designer: Robynne Raye
Printer: The Copy Co., Seattle, WA
Colors: Black, PMS Red on Simpson Evergreen Matte
Size: 18" by 24"

AAA Pawn Shop

Creating an ad campaign for a pawn shop is something of a challenge, as the images conjured up by such establishments are often less than positive. Mark Fuller, an art director at the The Martin Agency in Richmond, was well aware of the potential pitfalls involved in such a project, and managed to navigate between euphemistic white-washing and unpleasant reality in this series of posters for a local establishment.

"The posters convey the moody, sinister aspects of a pawn shop, but the feeling is counterbalanced by the friendly, 'tongue-in-cheek' nature of the copy and the facial expressions of the owner," Fuller says. The humorous, pithy headlines ("Patrons of pawn shops don't respond to long copy messages," Fuller deadpans) are further humanized by the use of a rich duotone for the photos of the owner, standing in front of gleaming merchandise. The strategy seems to have paid off. Reports Fuller, "the posters have helped generate an increase in floor traffic and sales."

Client: AAA Pawn, Richmond, VA
Agency: The Martin Agency, Richmond, VA
Art director: Mark Fuller
Copywriter: Tripp Westbrook
Photographer: Craig Anderson
Type designer: Owen Wachter/Just My Type, Richmond, VA
Printer: Spencer Printing Co., Richmond, VA
Colors: Black, blue, and red on Lustre-cream offset
Size: 19 1/4" by 31 1/4"

"My shop is like a bank. It's got a lobby, a safe, and an S.O.B. in the loan department."

"For some reason I've never had much of a problem with shoplifters."

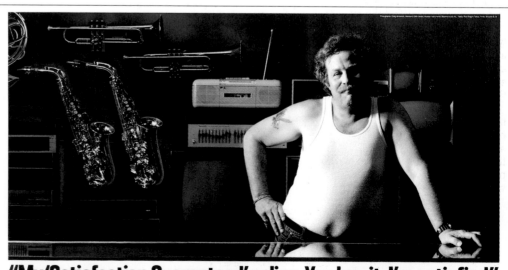

"My 'Satisfaction Guaranteed' policy: You buy it. I'm satisfied."

Dinosaur Valley

Rather than 65 million years in the making, this poster was completed in just three weeks. In the hopes of capitalizing on what was correctly anticipated to be a massive interest in dinosaurs, the Texas Department of Parks and Wildlife commissioned the Austin design firm of Fuller Dyal & Stamper to produce a piece that could be hung in the area's movie theater lobbies the week *Jurassic Park* opened (the claim to fame of the state park was its significant examples of dinosaur tracks).

"The theater lobby location suggested to us that the poster have maximum graphic impact, in the tradition of movie posters and marquees," says designer Herman Ellis Dyal. However, the intentionally sensationalistic graphic style caused a bit of a stir among Parks and Wildlife staff. "We created a design that challenged the conventional expectation of what a state park identity should be. The appropriateness of the proposed solution created lively discussion and debate within the department," Dyal recalls.

Although the poster (which was printed in an edition of 100) was hand-silkscreened, all other production for the piece depended on technology to enhance its appeal. The image of the dinosaur was scanned and manipulated in PhotoShop; "the type was found in an old type specimen book, scanned and cleaned up, then assembled with the image, support copy, and small logo in QuarkXPress," Dyal relates.

The poster has since become a collector's item, and park attendance has skyrocketed—"we'd like to think that was due, at least in part, to the poster," Dyal offers, with just a hint of sarcasm.

Client: Texas Department of Parks and Wildlife
Design firm: Fuller Dyal & Stamper, Austin, TX
Designer: Herman Ellis Dyal
Image manipulation/production: Ranulfo Ponce
Photographer: Paul Montgomery
Copywriter: Larry Fuller
Printer: Banner Sign Graphics
Colors: Red, yellow and black silkscreen
Size: 24" by 36"

Crosstie Walker Festival

"Crosstie Walker" is another name for a hobo, that particularly American folk icon whose surreptitious travels along the country's railroad lines during the Depression have been chronicled by everyone from Charlie Chaplin to John Steinbeck. The poster for the "Crosstie Walker Festival," held for the first time last year in Memphis, referenced this character to promote an effort on the part of the city to increase public awareness and traffic in a historic district under renovation near a series of train tracks.

Matt Young and Calvin Foster, principals of Royal Design, both live near the area in question, and agreed to help in its revitalization by designing the poster as a pro bono assignment. They made a special effort, both in the choice of woodcut-like illustration and antique display type, to underscore the fact that the area had historical significance. "We produced a silkscreened image with offset equipment, which made the poster look like it had a previous life. It not only gave the piece character; it also established the festival with a sense of validity," Young explains.

The extended vertical format was convenient for merchants in the area with limited display space, but also served an esthetic function: "We knew we had to romance the hobo as the central figure, so we designed the poster as an extreme vertical, enabling us to take an upward view, glorifying the character," Young says.

"The poster was received so well that merchants had to call for replacements because they were stolen," he says, and notes that the poster and related T-shirts are still selling briskly in shops throughout the district. "We have had requests for the poster from California to Boston to Australia. Most response has been with how the poster makes the viewer feel. That's nice."

Client: Crosstie Walker Festival, Memphis, TN
Design firm: Royal Design, Memphis, TN
Art directors/copywriters: Matt Young, Calvin Foster
Designer/letterer: Matt Young
Illustrator: Calvin Foster
Printer: Murdock Printing, Memphis, TN
Colors: PMS 420, PMS 185, PMS 875, black
Size: 12" by 34"

Matt Young and Calvin Foster, founders and principals of Royal Design in Memphis which started up in 1993, would like to be known as the Mssrs. Goodwrench of Tennessee design. "Roy and Al [the names of the two saluting service representatives in the poster] personify our accessibility and work ethic," Young says. "We actually do work side by side on each project, and feel we are practicing sound business methods combined with good, clean fun."

The poster's unusual horizontal orientation was a product of the pair's desire to use images that would convey their reliance on teamwork. "The use of nostalgic imagery was part of our efforts to inspire familiarity and trust," Young continues. They subsequently had the poster hand-screenprinted on a highly textured French Cordtone stock—"Sorta like the paper towels they clean your windshields with at the station," Young asserts.

The poster was a great success, and Young and Foster are happy with the results: "It's always more difficult to create an image piece for your own firm," Young claims. "But this turned out to be the perfect vehicle to introduce ourselves."

Client: Royal Design, Memphis, TN
Design firm: Royal Design, Memphis, TN
Art directors/copywriters: Matt Young, Calvin Foster
Designer: Matt Young
Illustrator: Calvin Foster
Printer: Serigraphics, Olive Branch, MS
Colors: Pantone Red, PMS 3155, PMS 141 and black on French Cordtone Cream Cover
Size: 38" by 14"

Between Boston and New York

When Connecticut Public Television was preparing the release of a documentary film that addressed the state's diverse population, economy, and culture, it chose Connecticut designer Peter Good to design a poster to promote the film.

Good was shown a preview of the documentary, whose title is "Between Boston and New York," and decided that a purely typographic treatment would be both simple and effective. "The idea was to show the diversity within the state by varying the style of letterforms," he relates. "The construction uses a variety of materials and techniques, including watercolor, painted wood, antique found letterforms, fabric wrapped around wood, and metal." Each letter evoked another aspect of Connecticut's identity, from its rich colonial history to its reputation as a manufacturing center.

The simplicity of the solution was echoed by a simplicity of production: "The photography was done as one shot, no retouching, no digital manipulation or color enhancement," Good states.

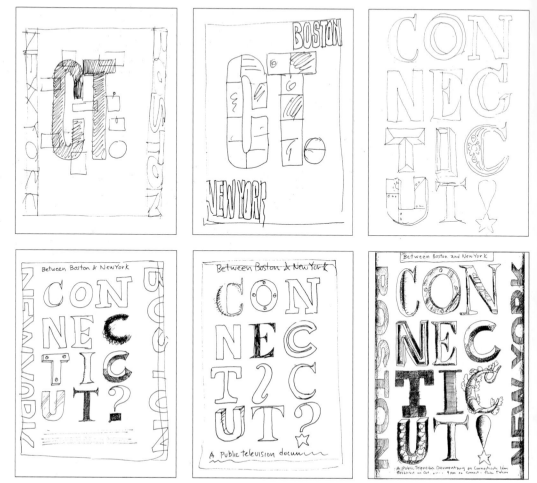

This page and opposite page, left: Good's preliminary layout and letter sketches.

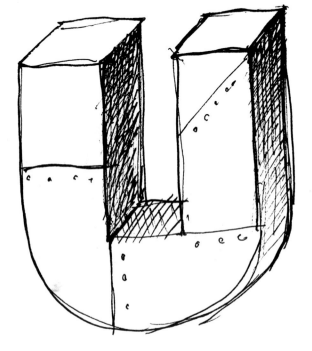

Client: Connecticut Public Television, Hartford, CT
Design firm: Peter Good Graphic Design, Chester, CT
Designer/illustrator: Peter Good
Copywriter: Larry Rifkin/CPTV
Photographer: Jim Coon
Printer: Actna Printing Services, Hartford, CT
Colors: 4-color process, black line art, and dull varnish on Warren's L.O.E. Dull Cover
Size: 24" by 38"

Although these posters have completely different themes and objectives, they are linked together in a significant way: Both were designed, lettered, and printed by Berkeley resident David Lance Goines.

Goines, who opened shop in 1965 as a printer (letter-press and photo-offset lithography, which is the method by which these posters were created), slowly transformed his practice from just printing other designers' work into producing his own. As he puts it, "I didn't mean to be a graphic designer; it just sort of happened that way."

Goines's "No War" poster was created as a personal response to what he calls "that incredibly stupid war," the Gulf War of 1991. The image of a darkened torso holding a skull is reminiscent of the powerful graphics of German expressionist Käthe Kollwitz, and the hand-lettering, which Goines based on the typeface Lithos, reinforces the timeless feeling of the piece. Goines printed it in an edition of 1000, sending most off to friends and associates who "either agreed or didn't agree with its message."

The other poster was commissioned by a Berkeley-area restaurant, Chez Panisse, as both a general promotion and an advertisement for a farmer's market street fair, where each of the restaurant's suppliers had an open stall from which fruit, vegetables, wine, and other comestibles could be sold to the public. The type, also hand-lettered by Goines, is based on the '20s typeface Neuland. Both

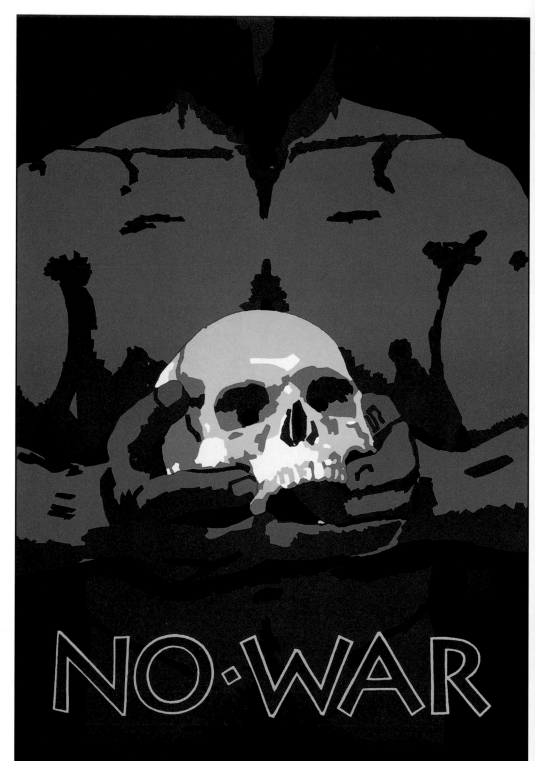

works are tour-de-force examples of photo-offset lithography—"No War" is composed of 7 solid colors; while "Farmers Market" was printed with 14.

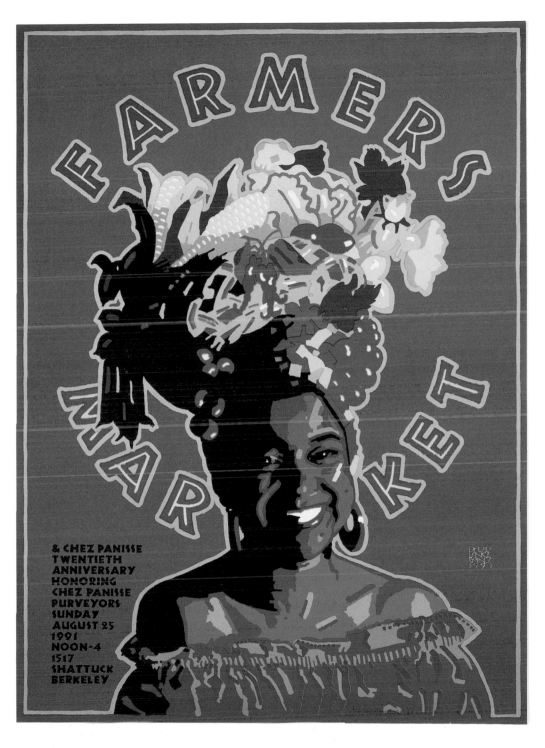

No War
Design firm: Saint Hieronymus Press, Berkeley, CA
Designer/printer: David Lance Goines
Colors: Seven solid colors on Mohawk Superfine 80-lb. Cover
Size: 17" by 24"

Farmers Market
Client: Chez Panisse, Berkeley, CA
Design firm: Saint Hieronymus Press, Berkeley, CA
Designer/printer: David Lance Goines
Colors: 14 solid colors on Mohawk Superfine 80-lb. Cover, soft white
Size: 17 5/8" by 24"

Great Ideas Never Happen Without Imagination

What possible relationship exists between images of a winding country road, Winston Churchill giving the "V" for victory, and the Eiffel Tower? Ask Paula Scher, designer of this arresting subway poster for New York City's School of Visual Arts, or, better yet, take a look at the poster itself. Scher relates, "I think it's obvious, but apparently a lot of people missed it: The initials *S*, *V*, and *A* are made by the images themselves."

In creating the poster, Scher had two goals in mind: to promote the school (hers is one of a series of posters for SVA designed by well-known creatives), and to execute a piece whose composition was almost solely computer-generated. "I thought that SVA should have a poster that was designed on computer," she says.

Like most work meant for the walls of the subway system, there was bound to be some sort of interactivity between designer and spectator. "On the Queens subway line, someone blacked out the forefinger on Churchill at every stop," she reports. No doubt a sign of hearty approval, New York style.

Client: School of Visual Arts, New York, NY:
Design firm: Pentagram, New York, NY
Creative director: Silas H. Rhodes
Designer: Paula Scher
Copywriter: Dee Ho
Electronic Imaging: Applied Graphics Technology, New York
Printer: Applied Graphics Technology
Colors: 4-color process
Size: 47" by 68"

Ask any designer for his or her definition of the plum assignment, and it will most certainly be one with a good budget, a generous schedule, and, best of all, a lot of creative latitude. All of these factors were present for Seymour Chwast when he was one of 45 designers asked to create a poster honoring Max Ponty, the designer of the Gitanes cigarette package. As he relates, "Since the poster was a celebration of the package and not intended for the public, it was possible to create a sophisticated design."

The blue Gitanes package, punctuated with the flowing figure of a flamenco dancer in shades of white, has been an icon in Europe for decades. The cigarette's manufacturer asked each designer to conjure the image of the dancer, as well as incorporating the "Gitanes" name into the poster layout. Chwast's charming and nostalgic solution calls to mind Art Nouveau posters of the early years of the century run through a Pushpin filter. However, he pays direct homage to Ponty by including a fairly literal version of the dancer's figure on the original package in the shadow extending underneath the left foot.

Client: Echo International, Paris, France
Design firm: The Pushpin Group, New York, NY
Art directors: Patrick Amsellem, Alain Weill
Designer/illustrator: Seymour Chwast
Printer: Graficaza, Paris, France
Colors: 4-color process
Size: 30" by 40"

A traveling exhibition of posters from the Soviet Union, sponsored by the America Institute of Graphic Arts, recently found its way to the AIGA's Cleveland headquarters, and that city's Watt, Roop & Co. were invited to design the poster announcing the event.

Art director Gregory Oznowich's main goal was to keep the piece simple and direct, and not only because of necessary financial restrictions. "Since the poster was to promote a design exhibit, we wanted to produce a poster that was simple, classic in style, bold in color and contrast, yet not so complicated as to detract from the posters in the show," he explains. His original solution involved the use of a hammer and sickle, but the AIGA chapter's exhibit committee felt it was too political. "The focus of the first design was too editorial, and took away from the message of the poster," he says. "We decided instead to interpret the title, 'A Window Into Soviet Life,' by using four rectangles, representing posters to form the shape of a window. The star symbolizes hope."

The extreme economy of form of the final design also lent itself well to other treatments: "The yellow field behind the red window could be expanded or reduced, affording us the flexibility we needed to make the transition from poster, to brochure, to other mediums and formats." Oznowich is especially pleased with the favorable response the piece engendered: "Even now, two years after the event, we still get requests for the poster based on its timelessness rather than its timeliness."

This page, and opposite page, top left: concept sketches show the design's progression from a more literal, informational solution to the simplified abstraction of the final design.

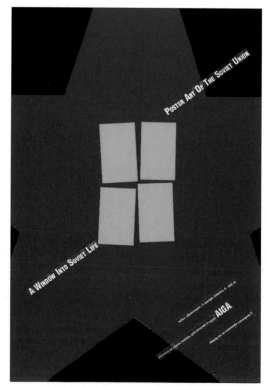

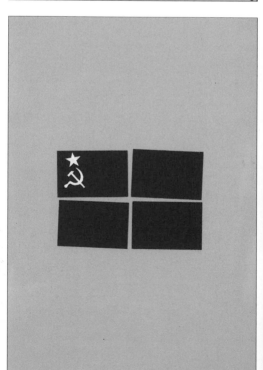

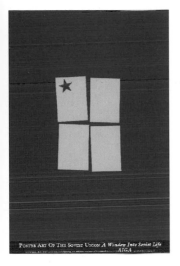

Client: AIGA, Cleveland Chapter, Cleveland, OH
Design firm: Watt, Roop & Co., Cleveland, OH
Art director/illustrator: Gregory Oznowich
Designers: S. Jeffrey Prugh, Mary Jane Parente/Smith
Printer: Fortran Printing, Cleveland, OH
Colors: Three PMS spot colors plus a gloss and dull varnish on Potlatch Vintage Gloss
Size: 21" by 31"

POSTER ART OF THE SOVIET UNION: A WINDOW INTO SOVIET LIFE

Presented by the Cleveland Chapter of the American Institute of Graphic Arts.

Monday July 29 through Friday August 23, at the Cleveland State University Art Gallery, 2307 Chester Avenue. Gallery hours: Monday through Friday 9:00 am to 5:00 pm.

AIGA

In 1991, Pentagram established the Pentagram Prize, a student competition whose winner is awarded with an internship at one of a number of highly regarded design firms. Pentagram New York partner John Klotnia has been responsible for the design of each year's poster announcing the event, which is sent to universities and art schools around the world.

As always, Klotnia was aware of the audience: "The poster was designed to appeal to a design-oriented group made up of students and professors," he explains. The theme of this year's contest was boundaries, and Klotnia felt the solution chosen best expressed that concept in the simplest, most graphic manner. "The use of type to define the boundary line demonstrated the theme clearly and succinctly." This wasn't, however, the designer's only solution. "I used the computer to refine my original sketches of the three ideas I developed; this one translated best," he relates, adding, "I think it was my best idea."

One reason he chose this idea was that it managed to evoke the theme without overdefining it: "Boundaries as a theme has many visual analogies. However, each of those other visuals might have led the competitors to follow too specific a path. I wanted to leave it more abstract but still representative of a boundary; type alone solved both problems." The poster's interchangeable format (it can be read either horizontally or vertically) only reinforced the subject matter.

Client: Pentagram Design Services, New York, NY
Design firm: Pentagram, New York, NY
Art director: John Klotnia
Copywriters: Jim Biber, Sarah Haun
Printer: Ambassador Arts, New York, NY
Films and separations: Typogram, New York, NY
Colors: PMS 485, black, and match creme on Mohawk Superfine
Size: 24" by 36"

Marie and Bruce

When Chicago's Parallax Theater staged a production of Wallace Shawn's *Marie and Bruce*, they called on designer Michael Bierut, who had initiated a poster series of that season's productions for the theater, to create the poster.

The designer's scatological solution was perfectly appropriate for the subject matter of the piece. "The play is a dark comedy about a married couple in a dysfunctional relationship. There is much profanity and abusive language. The poster image serves as an insider's reference to people who know the play," Bicrut explains, "and warns those who don't."

The theater identity (also designed by Bierut) is the only typeset element in the silkscreened poster, and runs along the top right side. The "stripped-down" (so to speak) black-and-white treatment of the piece is just right from a graphic standpoint, and suited the limited budget of the theater as well. The line drawing was executed by the designer, and the heart at the top of the handwritten text block as well as the emerging cupid silhouette were adapted from clip art. As Bierut concludes, "The director asked for something 'funny and shocking,' and I guess this fit the bill."

Client: Parallax Theatre Co., Chicago, IL
Design firm: Pentagram, New York, NY
Designer/illustrator/letterer: Michael Bierut
Printer: Ambassador Arts, New York, NY
Color: Black
Size: 24" by 36"

Collages de Oscar Mestey-Villamil

In September 1992, designer Oscar Mestey-Villamil designed a poster for an upcoming show of his new series of collages to be held in San Juan, Puerto Rico. The final design of the piece was arrived at by referencing a series of paintings Mestey-Villamil had done in the 1980s, but was finished, as Mesty-Villamil notes, "in the style I'm most comfortable with."

The simplicity and vibrancy of the poster was the result of his continual reworking of an arrangement of shapes, hand-lettering, and body type. Mestey-Villamil chose a larger size (approximately 25" by 40") for specific reasons: "I was interested in promoting the exhibition with a larger-than-average poster so the effect of colorful design could be enhanced." The visual, reminiscent of Matisse's "Jazz" cut-outs, exudes the colorful vitality of San Juan.

Mestey-Villamil recognizes the pleasure of designing a exhibition poster for his own work: "In this particular case, I knew exactly what I was looking for, so I just worked for it," he says. The poster was screen-printed, and hand-cut in an edition of 100, and has since been acquired by several international poster collections.

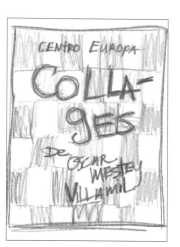

This page and opposite page, left: series of preliminary sketches by Mestey-Villamil.

Client: Oscar Mestey-Villamil,
San Juan, Puerto Rico
Designer: Oscar Mestey-Villamil
Printer: Taller en Blanco, San Juan,
Puerto Rico
Colors: Orange, red, and black on 36 lb.
Offset Ledger White
Size: 25 3/8" by 39 3/8"

Darkhorse Films

When Darkhorse Films asked the Slaughter-Hanson agency in Birmingham, Alabama, to design their first promotional poster/mailer, the production company's main concern was getting the attention of individuals and businesses in the region's creative community.

"We knew they wanted to create name awareness, as well as a bit of intrigue," says art director Marion English, adding, "They—and we—were hoping to create a piece that the recipients would hang in their offices." The resulting poster has exceeded expectations—besides garnering business for Darkhorse, Slaughter-Hanson has received a number of phone calls from individuals requesting copies. As English relates, "We see them hanging in offices, and even apartments, all over town."

Much of the piece's power comes from the haunting quality of the photograph, taken by Washington, DC-based Lisa Metzger. Metzger ended up donating the majority of the cost (the job's budget was very small); in return, she received promo posters with her name inserted—the result of a simple plate change at the printer. The depth of the photo was retained with the use of a tri-tone of double-dot black and a warm gray. "It really gave the piece the elegance we were looking for," says English.

DARKHORSE FILMS

Client: Darkhorse Films, Birmingham, AL
Design firm: Slaughter-Hanson, Birmingham, AL
Art director: Marion English
Photographer: Lisa Metzger, Washington, DC
Type designer: CA/Communication Arts, Birmingham, AL
Printer: American Printing, Birmingham, AL
Colors: Tri-tone on Cameo Dull 100-lb. Cover
Size: 38" by 25"

When the Dallas design firm Peterson & Co. first opened its doors back in 1985, Southern Methodist University was the fledgling concern's first client. As "a gesture of gratitude," principal Bryan Peterson has designed a series of pro bono posters for the school's annual book collecting contest. This one, from 1991, happens to be Peterson's personal favorite. "It is clever, and has an element of fun, while maintaining the level of sophistication a contest that involves book collecting should possess."

It was produced entirely on a Mac IIci with Adobe Illustrator. In fact, Peterson is inclined to share design credit with the software program: "The angled colored shapes that cut across the top curve of the portfolio and down the pages of the books were a result of failing to close the paths properly in Illustrator. This was a fortunate accident, and I feel that it enhances the design significantly." The series of curves in the illustration necessitated a mathematical equation to gradually slant the books down as they approached the spine. "I redrew the illustration no less than four times to achieve the proper visual perspective," he recalls.

Although the poster appears to have only two colors, it was in fact a five-color design, accomplished by the use of five different PMS inks. Peterson notes, "The poster is designed to go on a six-color press, so the only cost limitation is to make sure the poster can be printed in one pass." The richness and subtlety of the tones, combined with the strong graphic (the image was also used in newspaper ads and on the cover of the contest rules), made the poster a hot item on the SMU campus, literally—many of them were stolen, which might be regarded as the ultimate student compliment.

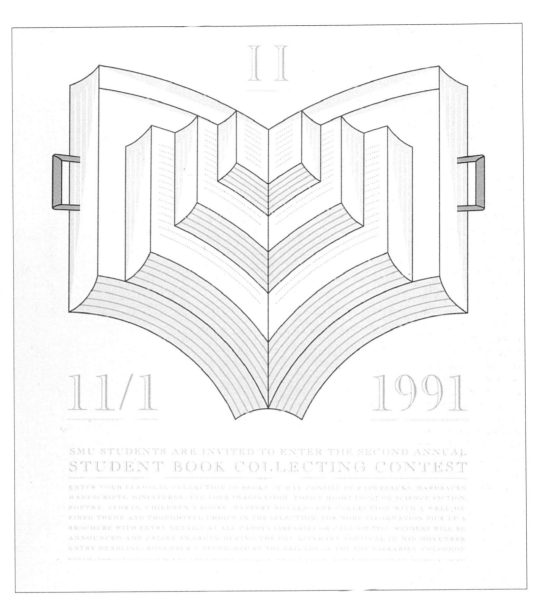

Client: Friends of the SMU Libraries, Colophon, Southern Methodist University, Dallas, TX
Design firm: Peterson & Co., Dallas, TX
Designer: Bryan L. Peterson
Printer: Padgett Printing, Dallas, TX
Colors: Five PMS colors on Proterra white 80-lb. Cover
Size: 23 1/2" by 26"

Seattle designer Art Chantry was confronted with the usual limitations of working for a non-profit organization when the city's Center on Contemporary Art, a regular client, approached him to design a poster for their performance series. "There was no budget to speak of—well, maybe $100," he recalls. Added to this were a tight schedule and vaguely impossible client requests (Chantry was asked to come up with a piece that would act as "a poster/flyer/handbill/media kit/attention-getting device and everything else"): in other words, the classic pro bono assignment. Although such projects can be incredibly frustrating, they often yield unexpectedly fresh design solutions, especially from someone as used to excelling in such an environment as Chantry.

The poster, which adopted the layout of a page from a tool catalog to list and advertise upcoming performance events at the Center, shares traits with much of Chantry's other work, namely a strong connection to vernacular design. Chantry heightened this effect by using two similar typefaces—Futura and Franklin Gothic—interchangeably throughout. "The resulting visual clash is virtually invisible to even the trained eye, but still gives the poster a 'clunk' or 'buzz' that you can't pinpoint. It drives people nuts." Printed in a silkscreen edition of 200, and a newsprint flyer edition of 5000, the poster, in Chantry's words, "got better reviews than the art it advertised."

This page: other mailers from the series Chantry designed for the Center on Contemporary Art.

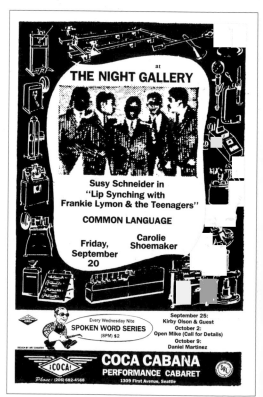

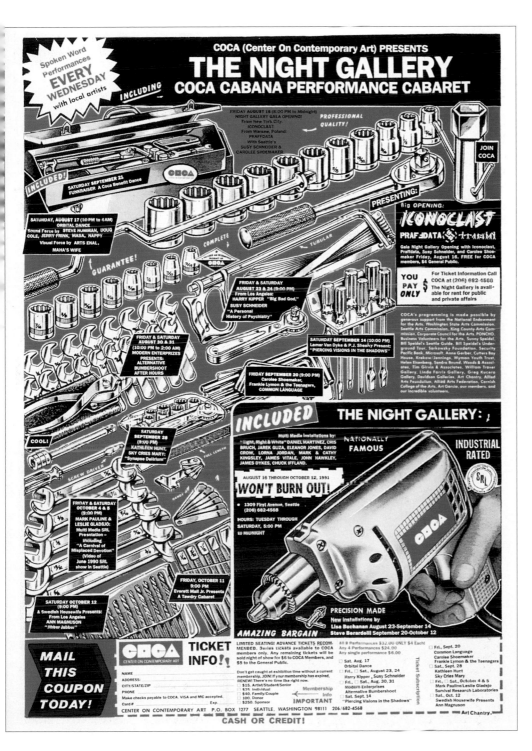

Client: Center On Contemporary Art (COCA), Seattle, WA
Designer: Art Chantry, Seattle, WA
Printer: Art Garcia, Seattle, WA
Colors: Red and black
Size: 22 3/4" by 31 1/2"

In 1991, the department of graphic design at the University of Industrial Arts in Helsinki, Finland, sent a "call for images" for an exhibition of faxes based on the theme "Just Now" to a number of designers and illustrators around the world. Pennsylvania designer Lanny Sommese happened to receive one of the calls.

"At that time, I was very interested in the breakup of the Soviet bloc countries and the resultant 'throttling down' of war machinery and tension on both sides," Sommese says. "I chose to do a sequence of related images that were transmitted to Helsinki two days apart, which meant that the process happened in real time." Each image was an economical line drawing of one type of war machine, fractured by a line. The first to be sent was that of a dissected plane, with the date 1991 positioned in the lower left-hand corner. In the next transmission, a split gun barrel was accompanied by the "19" and "91" separated into the top right- and left-hand corners. The third fax, depicting a cleaved missile, was sent with each of the four numbers in a corner. The progressive separation of the numbers was meant to further symbolize the dissolution of the Eastern Bloc.

At the exhibition, all of the contributions were displayed and subsequently printed in a catalog. Afterward, Sommese felt pleased enough with the series to produce it again in a larger format. Each was enlarged and silkscreened in-house in a limited edition of 50 copies. As Sommese explains, "I felt that they would translate into an arresting and timely series of posters that would, at the same time, symbolize and celebrate this remarkable and historical political event."

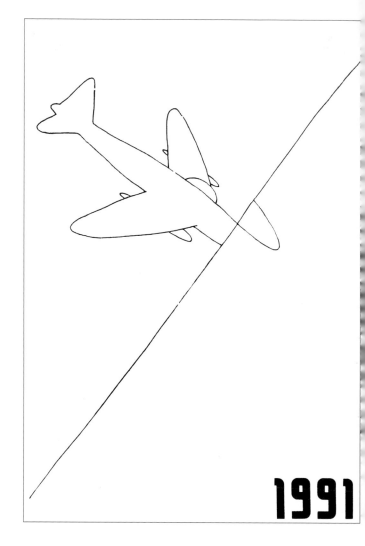

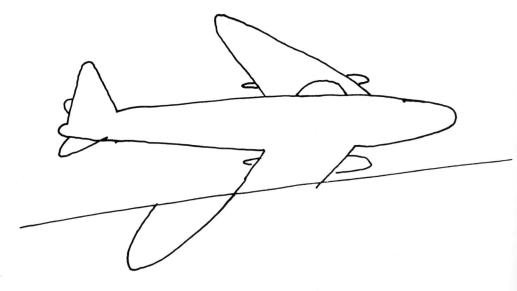

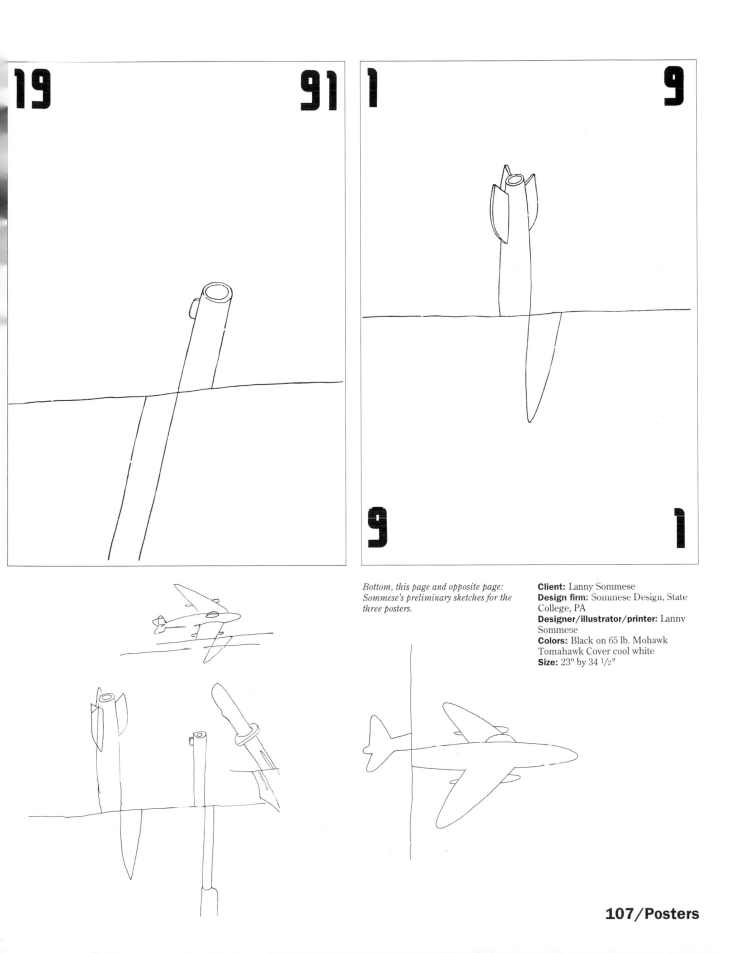

Bottom, this page and opposite page: Sommese's preliminary sketches for the three posters.

Client: Lanny Sommese
Design firm: Sommese Design, State College, PA
Designer/illustrator/printer: Lanny Sommese
Colors: Black on 65 lb. Mohawk Tomahawk Cover cool white
Size: 23" by 34 1/2"

Gene Federico

When Pentagram partner Michael Gericke was asked to design a poster for a talk by designer Gene Federico at the AIGA New York American Masters in Design series, he was clear on one thing: "It needed to be a very simple and graphic image."

Gericke was interested in evoking the clean, economical style of Federico, but also wanted to reference the well-known designer's work in an even more direct way. As Gericke explains, "For years, Gene has designed and sent his friends Christmas cards that use silhouettes of himself and his family." Gericke asked Federico to send along a black-and-white portrait of himself, along with a silhouette, and juxtaposed the two in a way that recalls Federico's own frequent meshing of two- and three-dimensional forms.

Because the project was a pro bono assignment, with the usual time and budget limitations—"I was given two weeks, from start to finish," Gericke recalls—he restricted the palette to two colors, black and red. The body copy, which runs in a clean line down the left hand side of the poster, is a mixture of the two colors, and was composed on the designer's Macintosh IIsi in QuarkXpress. "It was designed to be very dramatic," Gericke states.

Top: photographic portrait of Federico; above: one of Federico's Christmas cards which features silhouettes of himself, his wife, and their children.

Client: AIGA New York
Design firm: Pentagram, New York, NY
Designer/copywriter: Michael Gericke
Printer: Applied Graphic Technologies, New York, NY
Colors: Black and red on Mohawk Superfine white
Size: 24" by 36"